CARPE FREEDOM

PLAN YOUR FINANCIAL FUTURE
WHILE LIVING RICHLY TODAY

William Saoud & Aaron W. Saoud
SAOUD FINANCIAL

Copyright © 2020 by William Saoud and Aaron W. Saoud.

All rights reserved. No part of this publication may be reproduced, distributed, or transmitted in any form or by any means, including photocopying, recording, or other electronic or mechanical methods, without the prior written permission of the publisher, except in the case of brief quotations embodied in critical reviews and certain other noncommercial uses permitted by copyright law. For permission requests, write to the publisher at the address below. These materials are provided to you by William and Aaron Saoud for informational purposes only and William and Aaron Saoud and Advisors Excel, LLC expressly disclaim any and all liability arising out of or relating to your use of same. The provision of these materials does not constitute legal or investment advice and does not establish an attorney-client relationship between you and Bill and Aaron Saoud. No tax advice is contained in these materials. You are solely responsible for ensuring the accuracy and completeness of all materials as well as the compliance, validity, and enforceability of all materials under any applicable law. The advice and strategies found within may not be suitable for every situation. You are expressly advised to consult with a qualified attorney or other professional in making any such determination and to determine your legal or financial needs. No warranty of any kind, implied, expressed, or statutory, including but not limited to the warranties of title and non-infringement of third-party rights, is given with respect to this publication.

William Saoud and Aaron W. Saoud/Saoud Financial
21250 Hall Rd. Suite 300
Clinton Township, MI 48038

2202 N. Westshore Blvd., 2nd Floor,
Tampa, FL 33607

https://saoudfinancial.com/

Book layout ©2020 Advisors Excel, LLC

Carpe Freedom/William Saoud & Aaron W. Saoud. — 1st edition

ISBN 9798667136644

Aaron Saoud is registered as an Investment Advisor Representative, and William Saoud and Aaron Saoud are licensed insurance agents in the state of Michigan and Florida. Saoud Financial is an independent financial services firm that helps individuals create retirement strategies using a variety of investment and insurance products to custom suit their needs and objectives.

Investment advisory services offered only by duly registered individuals through AE Wealth Management, LLC (AEWM). AEWM and Saoud Financial, LLC are not affiliated companies. 622686

The contents of this book are provided for informational purposes only and are not intended to serve as the basis for any financial decisions. Any tax, legal, or estate planning information is general in nature. It should not be construed as legal or tax advice. Always consult an attorney or tax professional regarding the applicability of this information to your unique situation.

Information presented is believed to be factual and up-to-date, but we do not guarantee its accuracy, and it should not be regarded as a complete analysis of the subjects discussed. All expressions of opinion are those of the author as of the date of publication and are subject to change. Content should not be construed as personalized investment advice nor should it be interpreted as an offer to buy or sell any securities mentioned. A financial advisor should be consulted before implementing any of the strategies presented.

Investing involves risk, including the potential loss of principal. No investment strategy can guarantee a profit or protect against loss in periods of declining values. Any references to protection benefits or guaranteed/lifetime income streams refer only to fixed insurance products, not securities or investment products. Insurance and annuity product guarantees are backed by the financial strength and claims-paying ability of the issuing insurance company.

Any names used in the examples in this book are hypothetical only and do not represent actual clients.

This book is dedicated to Pat,
the loving wife and mother of the authors of this book.
We could not have written it without you.

"There's a time for daring and there's a time for caution, and a wise man understands which is called for."

Robin Williams, *Dead Poets Society*

Table of Contents

The Importance of Planning i
Longevity 1
    Retiring Later 3
    Health Care 4
    Long-Term Care 5
    Spousal Planning 15
Taxes 17
    The Fed 18
    Know Your Limits 18
    Assuming a Lower Tax Rate 19
    401(k)/IRA 20
Market Volatility 23
    The Color of Money 25
    Dollar-Cost Averaging 26
    Is There a "Perfect" Product? 28
Retirement Income 31
    Sources of Income 32
    Retirement Income Needs 34
    Other Expenses 38
    Putting It All Together 43
Social Security 47
    The Future of Social Security 47
    Full Retirement Age 50
    Spousal Benefits 54

    Taxes, Taxes, Taxes 58

    Working and Social Security: The Earnings Test 60

401(k)s & IRAs 63

    RMDs 69

    Roth 71

    Taking Charge 72

Annuities 73

    How You Get Paid 74

    Types of Annuities 76

    Other Things to Know About Annuities 79

Estate & Legacy 81

    Documents 82

    Taxes 87

Finding a Financial Professional by Bill Saoud 91

Women-Specific Concerns 95

    Be Informed 96

    Longevity 100

    Caregiving 103

Acknowledgments 107

About the Author 109

    William Saoud, President and CEO 109

    Aaron W. Saoud, Wealth Manager 109

FOREWORD
The Importance of Planning

The year 2020 started off riding the longest bull market in history, and we all watched as an unforeseen global pandemic put an end to that. Even those who had socked away hundreds of thousands of dollars felt the gut-check that accompanied the market drop as their retirement account balances fluctuated. Alternately, in our practice, we've seen people who, regardless of market performance, and regardless of how much they have saved, have their lives radically changed by the death of a spouse or a significant health event. Having your life and lifestyle dictated by your circumstances? That sure doesn't sound like freedom to us.

These experiences serve to underscore: Amassing money is not the same as planning for retirement because events—like the market correcting or a loved one passing—are outside of our control, but having a plan makes these things much easier.

When a plan is put together, our goal is not to just put money together in one place. The goal is to analyze the types of money our clients hold and take into account their dreams, goals, and plans for their retirement years. Then, understanding what money should be used—and when—allows us to advise clients on the appropriate process of income planning for their needs.

We know expenses are always going to happen—whether we plan for them or not! What is important to us, and to the folks we help every day, is we plan for the unexpected. As we always remind families, we hope for the best but plan for the worst.

A financial professional can help families create a plan by addressing the problems the clients are aware of—like how to ensure there is enough to pay the bills each month—but a good financial professional also prepares for the problems clients may be unaware they even have—like what *source* of money is the best to pay those bills, what resource is growing the most, or what asset is most susceptible to current market changes. As financial professionals, it is our job to prepare for the knowns, as well as the unknowns, that affect a family's life.

We believe our office is different from other offices in that we truly listen to our clients' goals. We want to understand what our clients want to do over the next year, five years, ten years, or more. Then, because we are independent, we are able to offer solutions as part of a financial plan that incorporates different financial companies and products to help our clients get where they want to go. At times, we see other financial offices under the umbrella of larger organizations are forced to offer only that particular company's products, which may not be really best for the family sitting in front of them, because they are forced to only offer one set of products.

Retirement can be challenging for a person or family without a plan. We know, with so much uncertainty in the world and so many things out of our control, it can be confusing for families who don't have a plan. Many of us know a friend or family member who was affected by previous downturns in the market or in the economy that have changed, or perhaps even ruined, their retirement plans. We know people who thought they were going to retire in 2009 or 2010, but, after the Great Recession, their entire dreams had to be altered. This is why having a plan is so important. A plan helps us weather those types of storms and stay on the right track to reach our goals.

We hope an income plan adds a sense of comfort, knowing a plan comes with clarity and direction. We know pilots would never take to the skies in a plane without a plan or a map. The same is true for families nearing retirement. A plan is essential to reach your destination with greater confidence.

CHAPTER 1

Longevity

You would think the prospect of the grave would loom more frightening as we age, yet many retirees say their number one fear is actually running out of money in their twilight years.[1] This fear is, unfortunately, justified, in part, because of one significant factor: We're living longer.

According to the Social Security Administration, in 1950, the average life expectancy for a sixty-five-year-old man was seventy-eight, and the average for a sixty-five-year-old woman was eight-one. In 2020, those averages were eighty-three and eighty-eight, respectively.[2]

The bottom line of many retirees' budget woes comes down to this: They just didn't plan to live so long. Now, when we are young and in our working years, that's not something we necessarily see as a bad thing; don't some people fantasize about living forever, or, at least, reaching the ripe old age of one hundred?

However, with a longer lifespan, as we near retirement, we face a few snags. Our resources are finite—we only have so much money to provide income—but our lifespans can be

---

[1] Samiha Khanna. Journal of Accountancy. February 14, 2019. "Clients' Top Fear: Running out of Money." https://www.journalofaccountancy.com/news/2019/feb/top-retirement-fears-201920387.html

[2] Social Security Administration. 2011 Trustees Report. "Actuarial Publications: Cohort Life Expectancy." https://www.ssa.gov/OACT/TR/2011/lr5a4.html

unpredictably long, perhaps longer than our resources allow. Also, longer lives don't necessarily equate with healthier lives. The longer you live, the more money you will likely need to spend on health care, even excluding long-term care needs like nursing homes.

You will also run into inflation. If you don't plan to live another twenty-five years but end up doing so, inflation at an average 2.5 percent will raise your $50,000-per-year budgeted need up to $93,000 per year. Or, if you live another eight years as inflation rises, you will need about $810,000 to cover those same expenses.[3] And this is before you count the expenses of any potential health care or long-term care needs.

Because we don't necessarily get to have our cake and eat it, too, our collective increased longevity hasn't necessarily increased the healthy years of our lives. Typically, our life-extending care most widely applies to the part of our lives where we will need more care in general. Think of a pacemaker at eighty-five, or radiation pills for cancer at seventy-eight.

"Wow, Bill and Aaron," We can hear you say. "Way to start with the good news first."

We know, we've painted a fairly grim picture. But all we're concerned about here is the cost. It's hard to put a dollar sign on life, but that is essentially what we're talking about when discussing longevity and your finances. According to the Stanford Center on Longevity, more than half of pre-retirees underestimate the life expectancy of the average sixty-five-year-old.[4] Living longer isn't a bad thing; it just costs more, and one key to a sound retirement strategy is preparing in advance for that expense.

One woman we know of illustrates this picture perfectly. Her mother passed away in her late seventies after years of suffering

---

[3] Katie Brockman. The Motley Fool. August 19, 2018. "More Americans are Living into Their 90s—and That's Bad News for Their Savings." https://www.fool.com/retirement/2018/08/19/more-americans-are-living-into-their-90s-and-thats.aspx

[4] Stanford Center on Longevity. "Underestimating Years in Retirement." http://longevity.stanford.edu/underestimating-years-in-retirement/

from Alzheimer's disease. Her father died at age eighty from cancer. With modern medicine and treatment, this woman survived two rounds of breast cancer, lived with diabetes, and endured a pacemaker, extending her life to age eighty-eight, nearly a decade beyond what she anticipated. However, she and her husband had saved and planned for "just in case," trying to be prepared if they had to move, needed nursing home care, or needed to help children and grandchildren with their expenses. One of their "just-in-case" scenarios was living much longer than they anticipated. The last six years of her life were fraught with medical expenses, but she was also blessed with knowing her five great-grandchildren and deepening relationships with her children and grandchildren. She was able to pay for her own medical care, including her final two years in a nursing home, and her twilight years were truly golden.

From age eighty-five to eighty-eight, she was more socially active, with many visits from family and friends, and she participated in more activities than she had in the seven years since her husband died. When she, too, passed away, her planning from decades earlier allowed her to pass on a legacy to her children. The legacy she left behind can be measured both in dollar signs *and* in other intangible ways.

Living longer may be more expensive, but it can be so meaningful when you plan for your "just-in-cases."

Retiring Later

Planning for a long life in retirement partly comes down to when you retire. While many people end up retiring earlier than they anticipated—due to injuries, layoffs, family crises, and other unforeseen circumstances—continuing to work past age sixty (and even sixty-five) is still a viable option for others and can be an excellent way to help establish financial comfort in retirement.

There are many reasons for this. For one, you obviously still earn a paycheck and the benefits accompanying it. Medical coverage and beefing up your retirement accounts with further savings can be pretty significant by themselves, but the advantage of continuing your income is also that it should keep you from dipping into your retirement funds, further allowing them the opportunity to grow.

Additionally, for many workers, their nine-to-five job is more than just clocking in and out. Having a sense of purpose can keep us active physically, mentally, and socially. That kind of activity and level of engagement may also help stave off many of the health problems that plague retirees. Avoiding a sedentary life is one of the advantages of staying plugged into the workforce, if possible.

We have one client, a gentleman who retired early (at age sixty-four), who later decided being home, day-in-and-out, was not something he could see himself doing for the remainder of his years. So, he decided to return to working full-time in order to give back and continue to serve, as he had for so many of his working years. He was extremely happy to get back to working, even at the age of sixty-six, because of what he was doing for others.

Health Care

Take a second to reflect on your health care plan. Although working up to or even past age sixty-five would allow you to avoid a coverage gap between your working years and Medicare, that may not be an option for you. Even if it is, when you retire, you will need to make some decisions about what kind of insurance coverage you may need to supplement your Medicare. Are there any medical needs you have that may require coverage in addition to Medicare? Did your parents or grandparents have any inherited medical conditions you might consider using a special savings plan to cover?

These are all questions that are important to review with your financial professional so you can be sure you have enough money put aside for health care.

Long-Term Care

Longevity means the need for long-term care is statistically more likely to happen. If you intend to pass on a legacy, planning for long-term care is paramount, since it's estimated that nearly 70 percent of Americans will need some type of it.[5] However, this may be one of the biggest, most stressful pieces of longevity planning we encounter in our work. For one thing, who wants to talk about the point in their lives when they may feel the most limited? Who wants to dwell on what will happen if they no longer can toilet, bathe, dress, or feed themselves?

We get it; this is a less-than-fun part of planning. But a little bit of preparation now can go a long way!

When it comes to your longevity, just like with your goals, one of the important things to do is sit and dream. It may not be the fun, road-trip-to-the-Grand-Canyon kind of dreaming, but spend time envisioning how you want your twilight years to look.

For instance, if it is important for you to live in your home for as long as possible, who will provide for the day-to-day fixes and to-dos of housework if you become ill? Will you set aside money for a service, or do you have relatives or friends nearby whom you would comfortably allow to help you? Do you have a preference for in-home care over a nursing home or assisted living? This could be a good time to discuss the possibility of moving into a retirement community versus staying where you are or whether it's worth moving to another state and leaving relatives behind.

These are all important factors to discuss with your spouse and children, as *now* is the best time to address questions and concerns. For instance, is aging in place more important to one spouse than the other? Are the friends or relatives who live

---

[5] Moll Law Group. 2019. "The Cost of Long-Term Care." https://www.molllawgroup.com/the-cost-of-long-term-care.html

nearby emotionally, physically, and financially capable of helping you for a time if you face an illness?

Many families we meet with find these conversations very uncomfortable, particularly when children discuss nursing home care with their parents. A knee-jerk reaction for many is to promise they will care for their aging parents. This is noble and well-intentioned, but there needs to be an element of realism here. Does "help" from an adult child mean they stop by and help you with laundry, cooking, home maintenance, and bills? Or does it mean they move you into their spare room when you have hip surgery? Are they prepared to help you toilet and bathe if that becomes difficult for you to do on your own?

We don't mean to discourage families from caring for their own; this can be a profoundly admirable relationship when it works out. However, we've seen families put off planning for late-in-life care based on a tenuous promise the adult children would care for their parents, only to watch as the support system crumbles. Sometimes this is because the assumed caregiver hasn't given serious thought to the preparation they would need, both in a formal sense and with regard to their personal physical, emotional, and financial commitments. This is often also because we can't see the future: Alzheimer's and other maladies of old age can exact a heavy toll. When a loved one reaches the point he or she is at risk of wandering away or needs help with two or more activities of daily living, it can be more than one person or family can realistically handle.

If you know what you want, communicate with your family about both the best-case and worst-case scenarios. Then, hope for the best, and plan for the worst.

Realistic Cost of Care

Wrapped up in your planning should be a consideration for the cost of long-term care. Although the majority of us will need some degree of long-term care—including the 30 percent of us who may need up to five years of facility care—60 percent of us underestimate the costs of nursing home care! On average, consumers underestimate the annual cost of a private room in a nursing home by 51 percent.[6]

Another piece of planning for long-term-care costs is inflation.

It's common knowledge prices have been and keep rising, and that will lower your purchasing power on everything from food to medical care. Long-term care is a big piece of the inflation-disparity pie, which is part of why many find their estimates of nursing home care widely miss the mark. According to one survey, people expected to pay around $25,350 in out-of-pocket long-term care expenses per year, but, in reality, they'll more likely be paying over $47,000.[7]

While local costs vary from state to state, here's the national median for various forms of long-term care (plus projections that account for 3 percent annual inflation, so you can see what we're talking about):[8]

---

[6] Tamara E. Holmes. Yahoo Finance. July 24, 2019. "Consumers Underestimate Costs of Long-Term Care."
https://finance.yahoo.com/news/consumers-underestimate-costs-long-term-173542918.html

[7] Moll Law Group. 2019. "The Cost of Long-Term Care."
https://www.molllawgroup.com/the-cost-of-long-term-care.html

[8] Genworth Financial. June 2018. "Cost of Care Survey 2018."
https://www.genworth.com/aging-and-you/finances/cost-of-care.html

	Home Health Care, Homemaker services	Adult Day Care	Assisted Living	Nursing Home (semi-private)
	Long-Term Care Costs: Inflation			
Annual 2017	$47,934	$18,200	$45,000	$85,775
Annual 2027	$64,419	$24,459	$60,476	$115,274
Annual 2037	$86,574	$32,871	$81,275	$154,919
Annual 2047	$116,348	$44,176	$109,227	$208,198

Fund Your Long-Term Care

One critical mistake we see are those who haven't planned for long-term care because they assume the government will provide everything. But that's a huge misconception. The government has two health insurance programs: Medicare and Medicaid. These can greatly assist you in your health care needs in retirement but usually don't provide enough coverage to cover all of your health care costs in retirement. Our firm isn't a government outpost, so we don't get to make decisions when it comes to forming policy and specifics about either one of these programs. We're going to give the overview of both, but, if you want to dive into the details of these programs, you can visit Medicare.gov and Medicaid.gov.

Medicare
Medicare covers those aged sixty-five and older and those who are disabled. Medicare's coverage of any nursing-home-related health issues is limited. It might cover your nursing home stay

if it is not a "custodial" stay, and it isn't long-term. For example, if you break a bone or suffer a stroke, stay in a nursing home for rehabilitative care, and then return home, Medicare may cover you. But, if you have developed dementia or are looking to move to a nursing facility because you can no longer bathe, dress, toilet, feed yourself, or take care of your hygiene, etc., then Medicare is not going to pay for your nursing home costs. [9]

Medicaid

Medicaid is a program the states administer, so funding, protocol, and limitations vary. Compared to Medicare, Medicaid more widely covers nursing home care, but it targets a different demographic than Medicare: those with low incomes.

If you have more assets than the Medicaid limit in your state and need nursing home care, you will need to use those assets to pay for your care. You will also have a list of additional state-approved ways to spend some of these assets over the Medicaid limit, such as pre-purchasing burial plots and funeral expenses or paying off debts. After that, your remaining assets fund your nursing home stay until they are gone, at which point Medicaid will jump in.

Some people aren't stymied by this, thinking they will just pass on their financial assets early, gifting them to relatives, friends, and causes so they can qualify for Medicaid when they need it. However, to prevent this exact scenario, Uncle Sam has implemented the look-back period. Currently, if you enroll in Medicaid, you are subject to having the government scrutinize the last five years of your finances for large gifts or expenses that may subject you to penalties, temporarily making you ineligible for Medicaid coverage.

So, if you're planning to preserve your money for future generations and retain control of your financial resources

---

[9] Medicare.gov. "What Part A covers." https://www.medicare.gov/what-medicare-covers/part-a/what-part-a-covers.html

during your lifetime, you'll probably want to prepare for the costs of longevity beyond a "government plan."

Self-Funding

One way to fund a longer life is the old-fashioned way, through self-funding. There are a variety of financial tools you can use, and they all have their pros and cons. If your assets are in low-interest accounts (savings, bonds, CDs), you risk letting inflation erode the value of your dollar. Or, if you are relying on the stock market, you have more growth potential, but you'll also want to consider the possible implications of market volatility. What if your assets take a hit? If you suffer a loss in your retirement portfolio in early or mid-retirement, you might have the option to "tighten your belt," so to speak, and cut back on discretionary spending to allow your portfolio the room to bounce back. But, if you are retired and depend on income from a stock account that just hit a downward stride, what are you going to do?

HSAs

These days, you might also be able to self-fund through a health savings account, or HSA, if you have access to one through a high-deductible health plan (you will not qualify to save in an HSA after enrolling in Medicare). In an HSA, any growth of your tax-deductible contributions will be tax-free, and any distributions paid out for qualified health costs are also tax-free. That can be a tax trifecta. Long-term care expenses count as health costs, so, if this is an option available to you, it is one way to use the tax advantages to self-fund your longevity. Bear in mind, if you are younger than sixty-five, any money you use for nonqualified expenses will be subject to taxes and penalties, and, if you are older than sixty-five, any HSA money you use for non-medical expenses is subject to income tax.

LTCI

One slightly more nuanced way to pay for longevity, specifically for long-term care, is long-term-care insurance, or LTCI. As car insurance protects your assets in case of a car accident and home insurance protects your assets in case something happens to your house, long-term care insurance aims to protect your assets in case you need long-term care in an at-home or nursing home situation.

As with other types of insurance, you will pay a monthly premium in exchange for an insurance company to pay for long-term care down the road. Typically, policies cover two to three years of care, which is adequate for an "average" situation: it's estimated 70 percent of Americans will need about three years of long-term care of some kind. However, it's important to consider you might not be "average" when you are preparing for long-term care costs; on average, 20 percent of today's sixty-five-year-olds will need care for longer than five years.[10]

Now, there are a few oft-cited components of LTCI that make it unattractive for some:

- Expense — LTCI can be expensive. It is generally less expensive the younger you are, but an average fifty-five-year-old couple who purchased LTCI in 2019 could expect to pay $3,050 each year for an average three-year coverage policy. And the annual cost only increases from there the older you are.[11]
- Limited options — Let's face it: LTCI is expensive for consumers, but it is also expensive for companies that offer it. With fewer companies willing to take on that expense, this narrows the market, meaning opportunities to price shop for policies with different options or custom benefits are limited.

---

[10] David Levine. *U.S. News*. July 10, 2019. "How to Pay for Nursing home Costs." https://health.usnews.com/best-nursing-homes/articles/how-to-pay-for-nursing-home-costs

[11] American Association for Long-Term Care Insurance. January 2019. "2019 National Long-Term Care Insurance Price Index." https://www.aaltci.org/news/wp-content/uploads/2019/01/2019-Price-Index-LTC.pdf

- If you know you need it, you may not be able to get it — Insurance companies offering LTCI are taking on a risk that you may need LTCI. That risk is the foundation of the product—you may or may not need it. If you know you will need it because you have a dementia diagnosis or another illness for which you will need long-term care, you will likely not qualify for LTCI coverage.
- Use it or lose it — If you have LTCI and are in the minority of Americans who die having never needed long-term care, all the money you paid into your LTCI policy is gone.
- Possibly fluctuating rates — Your rate is not locked in on LTCI. Companies maintain the ability to raise or lower your premium amounts. This means some seniors face an ultimatum: Keep funding a policy at what might be a less affordable rate or lose coverage and let go of all the money they paid in thus far.

After that, you might be thinking, "How can people possibly be interested in LTCI?" But let us repeat ourselves—as many as 70 percent of Americans will need long-term care. Those are pretty steady odds. And, although only 8 percent of Americans have purchased LTCI, keep in mind the costs of nursing home care. Can you afford $7,000 a month to put into nursing home care and still have enough left over to protect your legacy? This is a very real concern: One study says 72 percent of Americans are impoverished by the end of just one year in a nursing home.[12] So, not to sound like a broken record, but it is vitally important to have a plan in place to deal with longevity and long-term care if you intend to leave a financial legacy.

We absolutely believe all of our clients, who are suitable and have a need, should have a conversation about LTCI. It is worth, at a minimum, talking about in order to find out if there is a

---

[12] A Place for Mom. January 2018. "Long-Term Care Insurance: Costs & Benefits." http://www.aplaceformom.com/senior-care-resources/articles/long-term-care-costs.

need, and, if so, what options are available. We believe the more information an individual or family has after they leave our office, the better. Then, they can think on it, and, along with our guidance, decide what the right decision is for their family. There is rarely a situation in which, when a family needs it, they should not at least consider their LTCI options. While it will not be right for all those who come in, for the folks it is a good fit for, LTCI can really ease the burden of those eventual worries about health care expenses.

Product Riders

LTCI and self-funding are not the only ways to plan for the expenses of longevity. Some companies are getting creative with their products, particularly insurance companies. One way they are retooling to meet people's needs is through optional product riders on annuities and life insurance. Elsewhere in this book, we talk about annuity basics, and here's a brief overview: Annuities are insurance contracts. You pay the insurance company a premium, either as a lump sum or as a series of payments over a set amount of time, in exchange for guaranteed income payments. One of the advantages of an annuity is it has access to riders, which allow you to tweak your contract for a fee, usually about 1 percent of the contract value annually. One annuity rider some companies offer is a long-term-care rider. If you have an annuity with a long-term-care rider and are not in need of long-term care, your contract behaves as any annuity contract would—nothing changes. Generally speaking, if you reach a point when you can't perform multiple functions of daily life on your own, you notify the insurance company, and a representative will turn on those provisions of your contract.

Like LTCI, different companies and products offer different options. Some annuity long-term-care riders offer coverage of two years in a nursing home situation. Others cap expenses at two times the original annuity's value. It greatly depends. Some people prefer this option because there isn't a "use-it-or-lose-it" piece; if you die without ever having needed long-term care, you still will have had the income benefit from the base contract. Still, as with any annuities or insurance contracts, there are the usual restrictions and limitations. Withdrawing money from the contract will affect future income payments, early distributions can result in a penalty, income taxes may apply, and, because the insurance company's solvency is what guarantees your payments, it's important to do your research about the insurance company you are considering purchasing a contract from.

Understandably, a discussion on long-term care and its particulars is bound to feel at least a little tedious. Yet, this is a critical piece of planning for income in retirement, particularly if you want to leave a legacy.

In this instance, we can speak from the personal experiences of our family. Bill's father, as much as we love and respect him and as much advice as we have been able to offer him over the years, was stubbornly opposed to using any long-term care options. Now, you have to understand, his father is a member of the generation of men, who, even at advanced ages, still hold on to the tough and invincible stature they have occupied for much of their lives. So, when we suggested time-and-again he make some long-term care plans, he resisted.

A few years ago, he became quite sick, and he was at the point where we could not care for him in the way he needed. He ended up in a nursing home, having to use Medicare as his best option for paying for his stay there. Had he been able to use an LTCI policy, his choices and selection of available nursing homes, beds, and quality of care could have all been quite different and, perhaps, better. Fortunately, he was able to pull through his health crisis and, over time, was able to return home to his wife—but many nights passed while he was in the nursing home where we wished there was more we could do— more he wished we would have done.

His choice to not prepare for that type of situation, despite good advice he received from us and others, limited the available health care choices open and available to him. We are lucky and blessed to have had him recover as well as he did, and we think he learned a lot from the experience, as well.

Spousal Planning

Here's one thing to keep in mind no matter how you plan to save: Many of us will be planning for more than ourselves. Look back at all the stats on health events and the likelihood of long life and long-term care. If they hold true for a single individual, then the likelihood of having a costly health or long-term care event is even higher for a married couple. You'll be planning for not just one life but two. So, when it comes to long-term care insurance, annuities, self-funding, or whatever strategy you are looking at utilizing, be sure you are funding longevity for the both of you.

The people we know who are most successful when it comes to long-term care are those who plan ahead. For example, a could in good health in their early sixties would be wise to educate themselves about long-term care insurance. Getting a policy before you'll need it and when your health allows you to qualify, means you can get better benefits at a lower price. With how quickly the cost of health care is rising in the United States, seeing families prepare ahead of time for care is a relief, both for them personally and also for their kids and grandkids. This makes one less emotional burden for loved ones to carry if there is a health emergency in the future.

CHAPTER 2

Taxes

Where to begin with taxes? Perhaps by acknowledging we all bear responsibility for the resources we share. Roads, bridges, schools... It is the patriotic duty of every American to pay his or her fair share of taxes. Many would agree with me, though, while they don't mind paying their fair share, they're not interested in paying one cent more!

Now, just talking taxes probably takes your mind to April—tax season. You are probably thinking about all the forms you collect and how you file. Perhaps you are thinking about your certified public accountant or another qualified tax professional and saying to yourself, "I've already got taxes taken care of, thanks!"

However, what we see when people come into our office is that their relationship with their tax professional is purely a January through April relationship. That means they may have a tax professional but not a tax *planner*.

What we mean is tax planning extends beyond filing taxes. In April, we are required to settle our accounts with the IRS to make sure we have paid up on our bill or to even the score if we have overpaid. But real tax planning is about making each financial move in a way that allows you to keep the most money in your pocket and out of Uncle Sam's.

Now, as a caveat, we want to emphasize we are neither a CPA nor a tax planner, but we see the way taxes affect our clients, and we have plenty of experience helping clients implement tax-efficient strategies in their retirement income plans—in conjunction with their tax professionals.

The Fed

Now, in the United States, taxes can be a rather uncertain proposition. Depending on who is in the White House and which party controls Congress, we might be tempted to assume tax rates could either decline or increase in the next four to eight years accordingly. However, there is one (large!) factor we, as a nation, must confront: the national debt.

Currently, according to USDebtClock.org, we are over $20,000,000,000,000 in debt and climbing. That's $20 TRILLION with a "T." With just $1 trillion, you could park it in the bank at a zero percent interest rate and still spend more than $54 million every day for fifty years without hitting a zero balance.

Even if Congress got a handle and stopped that debt from its daily compound, divided by each taxpayer, we each would owe about $175,000. So, will that be check or cash?

Our point here isn't to give you anxiety. We're just saying, even with the rosiest of outlooks on our personal income tax rates, you cannot count on low tax rates for the long term. Instead, you and your network of professionals (tax, legal, and financial) should constantly be looking for ways to take advantage of tax-saving opportunities as they come. After all, the best "luck" is when proper planning meets opportunity.

So, how can we get started?

Know Your Limits

One of the foundational pieces of tax planning is knowing what tax bracket you are in based on your income after removing pre-tax or untaxed assets. Your income taxes are based on everything on which you have to pay taxes.

One reason to know your income tax rate is so you can see how far away you are from the next lower or higher tax bracket. This is particularly important when it comes to decisions, such as gifting and Roth IRA rollovers. You will want to be sure to talk to a tax professional and a financial advisor registered to provide investment advice prior to making any decisions.

For instance, based on the 2020 tax table, Mallory and Ralph's taxable income is just over $330,000, putting them in the 32 percent tax bracket and $3,400 above the upper end of the 24 percent tax bracket. They have already maxed out their retirement funds' tax-exempt contributions for the year. Their daughter, Gloria, is a sophomore in college. This couple could shave a considerable amount off their tax bill if they use the $3,400 to help Gloria out with groceries and school—something they were likely to do, anyway, but now can deliberately put to work for them in their overall financial strategy.

Now, we use Mallory and Ralph only as an example—your circumstances may be different—but we think this nicely illustrates the way planning ahead for taxes can save you money.

Assuming a Lower Tax Rate

Many people anticipate being in a lower tax bracket in retirement. It makes sense: You won't be contributing to retirement funds; you'll be drawing from them. And you won't have all those work expenses—work clothes, transportation, etc.

Yet, do you really plan on changing your lifestyle after retirement? Do you plan to cut down on the number of times you eat out, scale back vacations, and skimp on travel?

What we see in our office is many couples spend more in the first few years, or maybe the first decade, of retirement. Sure, later on, that may taper off, but usually only just in time for their budget to be affected by health and long-term care expenses. Do you see where this is going? Many people plan as though their taxable income will be lower in retirement and are surprised when the tax bills come in and look more or less the same as they used to. It's better to plan for the worst and hope for the best, wouldn't you agree?

401(k)/IRA

One sometimes unexpected piece of tax planning in retirement concerns your 401(k) or IRA. Most of us have one of these accounts or an equivalent. Throughout our working lives, we pay in, dutifully socking away a portion of our earnings in these tax-deferred accounts. There's the rub: tax-deferred. Not tax-free. Very rarely is anything free of taxation when you get down to it. Using 401(k)s and IRAs in retirement is no different. The taxes the government deferred when you were in your working years are now coming due, and you will pay taxes on the earned income from those accounts at whatever your current tax rate is.

Just to ensure Uncle Sam gets his due, the government also has a required minimum distribution, or RMD, rule. Beginning at age seventy-two, you are required to withdraw a certain minimum amount every year from your 401(k) or IRA, or else you will face a 50 percent tax penalty on any RMD monies you should have withdrawn but didn't—and that's on top of income tax.

Of course, there is also the Roth account. You can think of the difference between a Roth and a traditional retirement account as the difference between taxing the seed and taxing the harvest. Because Roths are taxed on the front end, there aren't tax penalties for early withdrawals of the principal nor are there taxes on the growth after you reach age fifty-nine-and-one-half. Perhaps best of all, there are no RMDs. Of course, you must own a Roth account for a minimum of five years before you are able to take advantage of all of its features.

This is one more area where it pays to be aware of your tax bracket. Some people may find it advantageous to "convert" their traditional retirement account funds to Roth account funds in a year they are in a lower tax bracket. Others may opt to put any excess RMDs from their traditional retirement accounts into other products, like stocks or insurance.

Does that make your head spin? Understandable. That's why it's so important to work with a financial professional and tax planner who can help you not only execute these sorts of tax-efficient strategies but also help you understand what you are doing and why.

Tax strategies within a plan are extremely important for the following reasons: They are one of the main foundations of a holistic financial and/or income plan. Without it, the income plan would not be a complete picture of what may occur during the clients' retirement years. Secondly, it shows the client what their tax rate is and where it will be during their income-producing years, as well as how a significant reduction in income can reduce and possibly maximize their tax obligation. Third, it will show the client what would happen when their (RMD) Required Minimum Distribution takes place at age seventy-two. This can be very important depending on whether or not they have taxable income. Furthermore, if the plan calls for a possible conversion from an IRA to a Roth IRA, this would be an additional reason for why a tax strategy is vitally important.

At Saoud Financial we have a strategic partnership with a wonderful accounting firm named Zotos & Associates. We have had a partnership with them for a number of years, and our clients have benefited from their expertise in helping us with some difficult situations. Mike, the owner, is a wonderful source of information when and if we need an immediate answer. Whenever we develop an income plan for our clients, it is extremely important to have their tax information be exact to protect their income from fluctuations. It is comforting to know we can call on our strategic tax partner for answers to complicated tax scenarios. The tax strategies we put into all our clients' income and financial plans have to make sense to them and be as accurate as we can make them, all while still being understandable. Zotos & Associates help us with that part of it.

It cannot be overstated that planning for taxes is one of the most important parts of an income plan. For example, if a client moves any of her existing investments from one vehicle to another, we have to make sure it doesn't trigger a tax event. The client may end up owing taxes to the IRS if such a move is not done correctly.

Three examples of how important planning for taxes can be are as follows: First, how will the income they will be receiving in retirement affect their tax bracket? Second, how will their Required Minimum Distribution (RMD) affect their overall income and specific tax bracket? Third, how will a conversion of an IRA to a Roth IRA impact their income and taxes? These are all very important questions that should be addressed at the time of creating an income plan, along with the incorporation of a tax plan.

CHAPTER 3

Market Volatility

Up and down. Roller coaster. Merry-go-round. Bulls and bears. Peak-to-trough.
Sound familiar? This is the language we use to talk about the stock market. With volatility and spikes, even our language is jarring, bracing, and vivid.

Still, financial strategies tend to revolve around market-based products because there is no other financial class that packs the same potential for growth, pound for pound, as stock-based products. Because of growth potential, inflation protection, and new opportunities, it may be unwise to avoid the market entirely.

However, along with the potential for growth is the potential for loss. Many of the people we see in our office come in still feeling a bit burned from the market drama of 2000 to 2010. That was a rough stretch.

So how do we balance these factors? How do we try to satisfy both the need for protection and the need for growth?

For one thing, it is important to recognize the value of diversity. Now, we're not just talking about the diversity of assets among different kinds of stocks, or even different kinds of stocks and bonds. That's only one kind of diversity; while important, both stocks and bonds, though different, are still market-based products. Just as an incoming tide raises all boats, most market-based products tend to rise or lower as a whole, so diversity among stocks and bonds won't protect your assets during times when the market as a whole is in decline.

Therefore, a portfolio diverse in only market-sourced products won't automatically protect your assets during times when the market declines.

In addition to the sort of "horizontal diversity" you have by purchasing a variety of stocks and bonds from different companies, we encourage having "vertical diversity," or diversity among asset classes. This means having different product types—with varying levels of growth potential, liquidity, and principal protection—all in accordance with your unique situation, goals, and needs. And while diversification can't guarantee a profit or that you won't lose money in a down market, it is still an effective way to help smooth out market volatility within your portfolio.

Market volatility is something we talk about often in our office, and it is something we believe clients are usually aware of. Undoubtedly, the media throws all kinds of market volatility statistics in the faces of their audience, and sometimes the media can scare folks into believing they are not on the right financial path. Our take, using something called the "Rule of 100" as a starting point, is that clients should look at their age and keep about that much of their money protected, with the remainder adding up to 100. The remainder of the money should be placed in assets that experience market ups and downs.

For example, if we take a sixty-year-old, according to the "Rule of 100," this person should have around 60 percent of their money in a place where the principle cannot be lost. The remaining amount, 40 percent (totaling up to 100 percent) can possibly be invested in a place with more upside reward—with the associated risk that comes with it.

We use the "Rule of 100" as a general guideline although every family that comes into our office is different. For some, the Rule of 100 will not apply or be appropriate. Considerations on how and when to use the Rule of 100 will depend on the client's age, net worth, expenses, and future plans and goals. As with anything, whether a diet or workout routine, there is no one-size-fits-all approach, though there are general guidelines most professionals would agree on—in fitness as well as in finance. The key is then to take the guideline and customize how it might work for a particular family based on some of the factors we listed above.

The Color of Money

When you're looking at your overall portfolio diversity, part of the equation is knowing which products fit into which category: what has liquidity, what has protection, and what has growth potential.

Before we dive in, keep in mind these aren't absolutes. You might think of liquidity, growth, and protection as primary colors. While some products will look pretty much yellow, red, or blue, others will have a mix of characteristics, making them more green, orange, or purple.

Growth

We like to think of the growth category as red. It's powerful, it's somewhat volatile, and it's also the category where we have the greatest opportunity for growth and loss. Often, products in the growth category will have a good deal of liquidity but very little protection. These are our market-based products and strategies, and we think of them mostly in shades of red and orange, to designate their growth and liquidity. This is a good place to be when you're young—think fast cars and flashy leather jackets—but its allure often wanes as you move closer to retirement. Examples of "red" products include:
- Stocks
- Equities
- Exchange-traded funds
- Mutual funds
- Corporate bonds
- Real estate investment trusts

- Speculations
- Alternative investments

Liquidity

Yellow is our liquidity category color. We typically recommend having at least enough yellow money to cover six months' to a year's worth of expenses in case of emergency. Yellow assets don't need a lot of growth potential; they just need to be readily available when we need them. The "yellow" category includes:
- Cash
- Money market accounts

Protection

The color of protection, to me, is blue. Tranquil, peaceful, sure, even if it lacks a certain amount of flash. This is the direction we like to see people move toward as they're nearing retirement. The red, flashy look of stock market returns and the risk of possible overnight losses can be less attractive as we near retirement and look for more consistency and reliability. While this category doesn't come with a lot of liquidity, the products here are backed by an insurance company, a bank, or a government entity. "Blue" products include:
- Certificates of deposit—FDIC-insured
- Government-based bonds—backed by the full faith of the U.S. government
- Life insurance—backed by the financial strength of the issuing company
- Annuities—backed by the financial strength of the issuing company

Dollar-Cost Averaging

With 401(k)s and other market-based retirement products (IRAs, 403(b)s, etc.), when you are investing for the long term, the concept of dollar-cost averaging can be an effective tool. When the market is trending up, if you are consistently paying in money, month over month, great; your investments have the opportunity to grow, and you are adding to your assets. When the market takes a dip, no problem; your dollars buy more shares at a lower price. At some point, the market will likely increase, in which case your shares could be more valuable than they were before. This phenomenon is what we call dollar-cost averaging. And while it doesn't ensure a profit or guarantee against loss, it can be an effective way of maintaining an investment discipline and letting market volatility work for you.

However, when you are in retirement, this strategy may work against you. You may even hear of the term "reverse" dollar-cost averaging. Before, when the market lost ground, you were bargain-shopping; your dollars purchased more assets at a reduced price. When you are in retirement, you are no longer the purchaser; you are selling. So, in a down market, you have to sell more assets to make the same amount of money as you did in a favorable market.

We've had lots of people step into our office saying, "My advisor says the market always bounces back, and I just have to hold on for the long term."

There's truth in that. Thus far, the market has always rebounded to higher heights than before. But the prospect of potentially higher returns in five years may not be very helpful in retirement if you are relying on the income from those returns, for example, to pay this month's electric bill. That's why, at our firm, we specialize in insurance strategies that help provide a reliable stream of income.

Insurance products, like certain annuities, can be extremely useful in providing reliable income in retirement because insurance products are typically less risky than the stock market, overall. Often, insurance carriers will also provide certain guarantees within their products in order to allow families to be able to count on income, either immediately or down the road, and throughout retirement.

It is common for us to discuss insurance products as possible income sources for families—they can be really great complements to social security income, pensions, and stock dividends. All of these income-producing items will allow families a less worrisome, more confident outlook on their retirement because they can count on the income being there. And, it goes without saying, having a diversified portfolio of income-producing assets and investments makes for a well-rounded financial picture.

Is There a "Perfect" Product?

To bring us back around to the discussion of protection, growth, and liquidity, the ideal product would be a "ten" in all three categories, right? Completely guaranteed, doubling in size every few years, and accessible whenever you want. Does such a product exist? Anyone who says, "yes" is either ignorant or malevolent.

Instead of running in circles looking for that perfect product—the silver bullet, the unicorn of financial strategies—it's more important to circle back to the concept of a balanced, asset-diverse retirement portfolio.

This is why your interests may be best served when you work with a team of qualified financial professionals who know what various financial products can do and how you can use them in your personal retirement plan.

We believe avoiding volatility is really important—the long-term effects of market volatility on a portfolio can really be dramatic. We have seen it firsthand, sadly, with families coming to us after a major downturn has occurred and needing help—and, while we are so happy to be able to help, if we could only have seen them before the downturn, there might have been so much more we could have done.

Likewise, we feel it is important to plan for inflation—the rising costs of things (milk, bread, cars, etc.). We cannot hope to just avoid the volatility of the market by entirely sitting on the sidelines and not having available options or vehicles for making our money grow. Growth is important, so we have to help folks find more conservative, or less risky, ways of growing some of their money to keep pace with inflation. Otherwise, due to inflation, we are essentially losing money by not achieving growth.

CHAPTER 4

Retirement Income

Retirement. For many of us, it's what we've saved for and dreamed of, pinning our hopes to a magical someday. Is that someday filled with traveling? Spoiling the grandkids? Gardening? Maybe your fondest dream is just never having to work again, never having to clock in or be accountable to someone else.

Your ability to do these things all hinges on *income*. Without the money to support these dreams, even a basic level of work-free lifestyle is unsustainable. That's why planning for your income in retirement is so foundational. But where do we begin?

It can be easy to feel overwhelmed by this question. Some may feel the urge to amass a large lump sum and then try to put it all in one product—insurance, investments, liquid assets—to provide all the growth, liquidity, and income they need. Instead, we think you need a more balanced approach. After all, retirement planning isn't magic. There is no single product that can be all things to all people (or even all things to one person), and no approach works unilaterally for everyone. That's why it's important to talk to a financial professional who can help you lay down the basics and take you step by step through the process. Not only will you have the assurance you have addressed the areas you need to, but you will also have an ally who can help you break the process down and help keep you from feeling overwhelmed.

Sources of Income

Thinking of all the pieces of your retirement expenses might be intimidating. But, like cleaning out a junk drawer or revisiting that garage remodel, once you have laid everything out, you can begin to push things into categories.

Once you have a good overall picture of where your expenses will lie, you can start stacking up the resources to cover them.

Social Security

Social Security is a guaranteed, inflation-protected federal insurance program playing a significant part in most of our retirement plans. From delaying until you've reached full retirement age or beyond to examining spousal benefits, as we discuss elsewhere in this book, there is plenty you can do to try to make the most of this monthly benefit. As with all of your retirement income sources, it's important to see how to make this resource stretch to help provide the most bang and buck for your situation.

Pension

Another generally reliable source of retirement income for you might be a pension, if you are one of the lucky people who still has one.

If you don't have a pension, go ahead and skim on down to the next point, but, if you do have a pension, let's take a second to take a closer look.

Because your pension can be such a central piece of your retirement income plan, you will want to put some thought into answering basic questions about it.

How well is your pension funded? Since the heyday of the pension, companies and governments have neglected to fund their pension obligations, causing a persistent problem with this otherwise reliable asset. A report by the American

Legislative Exchange Council revealed a $5.96 trillion deficit in state pension funds overall in 2018.[13] Is your pension one of those?

In addition to checking up on your pension's health, check into what your options are for taking your pension. If you have already retired and made those decisions, this may be a foregone conclusion. If not, it pays to know what you can expect and what decisions you can make, such as taking spousal options to cover your husband or wife if he or she outlives you.

Also, some companies are incentivizing lump-sum payouts of pensions to reduce the companies' payment liabilities. If that's the case with your employer, talk to your financial professional to see if it might be prudent to do something like that or if it might be better to stick with lifetime payments or other options.

Your 401(k) and IRA

The "modern way" to save for retirement is in a 401(k) or IRA (or their nonprofit and governmental equivalents). These tax-advantaged accounts are, overall, a poor substitute for pensions, but one of the biggest disservices we do to ourselves in our working years is to not take full advantage of them in the first place. According to one article, about 42 percent of adults under thirty and 26 percent of adults thirty to forty-four haven't contributed to any retirement account, let alone their 401(k). [14]

Also, if you have changed jobs over the years, do the work of tracking down any benefits from your past employers. You

---

[13] Jonathan Williams, Christine Smith, Thurston Powers, and Bob Williams. ALEC. March 20, 2019. "Unaccountable and Unaffordable 2018." https://www.alec.org/publication/unaccountable-and-unaffordable-2018/

[14] Niall McCarthy. Forbes. June 3, 2019. "Report: A Quarter of Americans Have No Retirement Savings." https://www.forbes.com/sites/niallmccarthy/2019/06/03/report-a-quarter-of-americans-have-no-retirement-savings-infographic/#5fb35b703ebf

might have an IRA here or a 401(k) there; keep track of those so you can pull them together and look at those assets when you're ready to look at establishing sources of retirement income.

Other Assets

- Do you have life insurance?
- Do you have any annuities?
- How about long-term care insurance?
- Any passive income sources?
- Stock and bond portfolios?
- Liquid assets? (What's in your bank account?)
- Any alternative investments?
- Rental properties?

It's important, if you are going through the work of sitting with a financial professional, to look at your retirement income picture and pull together *all* of your assets, no matter how big or small. From the free insurance policy offered at your bank to the sizable investment in your brother-in-law's modestly successful furniture store, you want to have a good idea of where your money is.

We had one woman in her late fifties come into our office, and she was totally surprised by how much she had in assets once we put everything together for her. How nice when something unexpected like that happens! Her plan showed her, although things were split up in various sources and investments, she had a lot more than she realized. And her story isn't totally unique either—we see this quite often.

Retirement Income Needs

How much income will you need in retirement? How do you determine that? A lot of people work toward a random number, thinking, "If I can just have a million dollars, I'll be comfortable in retirement!" Don't get us wrong; it is possible to save up a lot of money and then retire in the hopes you can keep your monthly expenses lower than some set estimation. But we think this carries a general risk of running out of money. Instead, we work with our clients to find out what their current and projected income needs are and then work from there to see how we might cover any gaps between what they have and what they want.

Goals and Dreams

We like to start with your pie in the sky. Do you find yourself planning for your vacations more thoroughly than you do your retirement? A recent survey found one in five Americans spend more time planning our vacations than we spend planning our retirements.[15] Maybe it's because planning a vacation is less stressful: Having a week at the beach go awry is, well, a walk on the beach compared to running out of money in retirement. Whatever the case, perhaps it would be better if you thought of your retirement as a vacation in and of itself—no clocking in, no boss, no overtime. If you felt unlimited by financial strain, what would you do?

Would an endless vacation for you mean Paris and Rome? Would it mean mentoring at children's clubs or serving at the local soup kitchen? Or maybe it would mean deepening your ties to those immediately around you—neighbors, friends, and family. Maybe it would mean more time to do hobbies and activities you love. Have you been considering a second (or even third) act as a small business owner, turning a hobby or passion into a revenue source?

This is your time to daydream and answer the question: If you could do anything, what would you do?

---

[15] Malika Mitra. CNBC. August 2, 2019. "You're not alone if you spend more time planning your vacation than working on your finances." https://www.cnbc.com/2019/08/02/1-in-5-people-spend-more-time-planning-vacations-than-finances-survey.html

After that, it's a matter of putting a dollar amount on it. What are the costs of round-the-world travel? One couple we know said their highest priority in retirement was being able to take each of their grandchildren on a cross-country vacation every year. That's a pretty specific goal—one that is reasonably easy to nail down a budget for.

One couple who works with us dreamed of buying an RV to travel the whole United States. They had it in their minds a trip across the country would be a bucket-list fulfillment of a lifelong dream . . . and it really was for them! Now, they are planning their next big adventure—a similar road trip, but through Canada this time. They had so much fun doing it the first time, they decided to try it again.

Current Budget

A current expense report is one of the trickiest pieces of retirement spending. Most people assume the expenses of their lives in retirement will be different—lower. After all, there will be no drive to work, no need to keep a formal wardrobe, and, perhaps most impactful of all, no more saving for retirement!

Yet, we often underestimate our daily spending habits. That's why we typically ask our clients to bring in their bank statements for the past year—they are reflective of your *actual* spending, not just what you think you're spending.

We always sit down with our clients and go over all of their bills and expenses to help them see a tangible picture of where they are at financially. It usually ends up being a pretty eye-opening experience for them, to see where their money is going, and it helps them realize how much they are spending—or how much they may need in the future.

We can't count the number of times we have sat with a couple, asked them about their spending, and had them throw out a number that seemed incredibly low. When we ask them where the number came from, they usually say they estimated based on their total bills. Yet, our spending is so much more than our mortgage, utilities, cable, phone, car, grocery, or credit card bills.

"What about clothes?" we ask, "Or dining out? What about gifts and coffees and last-minute birthday cards?" That's when the lights come on.

This is why we suggest collecting a year's worth of information. There is usually no such thing as a one-time purchase. Did you buy new furniture? Even if that is a rarity, do you think that will be the last time you *ever* buy furniture?

We had a family come in last year who we remember so distinctly because of how nice and friendly the family, with two kids in high school, was. They sat down with us and told us what their estimated expenses were, but they were also deeply concerned because they felt like they were falling further and further behind on their bills. When we ran their expense calculation—taking into account all the different activities and outgoing money they spent on a monthly basis—we discovered they were actually spending twice as much as they had originally thought they were.

These days, it is so easy to forget about all of the recurring subscriptions and small miscellaneous things that add up over time. It is an interesting time because never before have families had to worry about all of their internet and streaming services. It was unheard of before the present times. Today, families must take into consideration Netflix, Verizon, Disney+, Hulu, Amazon, and all of the other possible services that pop up every couple of years. In fact, by the time you read this, there may even be the newest, latest-and-greatest service being offered as the latest "must-have" for families. Of course, this is how these large corporations make their money and expand so quickly. As consumers, we have to consider how each of these music, video, and various other amenities affect our bottom-line. In essence, this is why that particular family had under-projected their expenses by nearly half!

Another hefty expense is spending on the kids. Many of the couples we work with are quick to help their adult children, whether it's something like letting them live in the basement, paying for college, babysitting, paying an occasional bill, or even just contributing to a grandchild's college fund. They aren't alone—79 percent of Americans in 2018 said they had provided financial support for an adult child. And it's not unlikely for some parents to tap into their retirement funds to do so.[16]

My clients sometimes protest what they do for their grown children can stop in retirement. They don't *need* to help. But we get it. Parents like to feel needed. And, while you never want to neglect saving for retirement in favor of taking on financial risks (like your child's student debt), the parents who help their adult children do so in part because it helps them feel fulfilled.

When it comes down to expenses, including (and especially) spending on your family, don't make your initial calculations based on what you *could* whittle your budget down to if you *had* to. Instead, start from where you are. Who wants to live off a bare-bones bank account in retirement?

Other Expenses

Once you have nailed down your current budget and your dreams or goals for retirement, there are a few other outstanding pieces to think about—some expenses many people don't take the time to consider before making and executing a plan. But we assume you want to get it right, so let's take a look.

---

[16] Lorie Konish. CNBC. October 2, 2018. "Parents Spend Twice as Much on Adult Children than They Save for Retirement."
https://www.cnbc.com/2018/10/02/parents-spend-twice-as-much-on-adult-children-than-saving-for-retirement.html

Housing

Do you know where you want to live in retirement? This makes up a substantial piece of your income puzzle—since the typical American household owns a home, and it's generally their largest asset—but it often goes unaccounted for until the last minute. [17]

Some people prefer to live right where they are for as long as they can. Others have been waiting for retirement to pull the trigger on an ambitious move. Whatever your plans and whatever your reasons, there are quite a few things to consider.

Mortgage

Do you still have a mortgage? What may have been a nice tax boon in your working years could turn into a financial burden in your retirement. After all, when you are on a limited income, a mortgage is just one more bill sapping your financial strength. It is something to put some thought into, whether you plan to age in place or are considering moving to your dream home, buying a house out of state, or living in a retirement community.

Upkeep and Taxes

A house without a mortgage still requires annual taxes. While it's tempting to think of this as a once-a-year expense, when you have limited earning potential, your annual tax bill might be something into which you want to put a little more forethought.

The costs of homeownership aren't just monetary. When you find yourself dealing with more house than you need, it can drain your time and energy. From keeping clutter at bay to keeping the lawn mower running, upkeep can be extensive and expensive. For some, that's a challenge they heartily accept and

---

[17] Jann Swanson. Mortgage News Daily. August 28, 2019. "Homeownership is the Top Contributor to Household Wealth." http://www.mortgagenewsdaily.com/08282019_homeownership.asp

can comfortably take on. For others, the idea of yard work or cleaning an area larger than they need feels foolish.

For instance, Peggy discovered after her knee replacement that most of her house was inaccessible to her when she was laid up.

"It felt ridiculous to pay someone else to dust and vacuum a house I was only living in 40 percent of!"

Practicality and Adaptability

Erik and Magda are looking to retire within the next two decades. They just sold their old three-bedroom ranch-style house. Their twins are in high school, and the couple has wanted to "upgrade" for years. Now they live in a gorgeous 1940s three-story house with all the kitchen space they ever wanted, five sprawling bedrooms, and a library and media room for themselves and their children. Within months of moving in, the couple realized a house perfect for their active teens would no longer be perfect for them in five to fifteen years.

"We are already paying the mortgage for this house, but we've started saving for the next one," said Magda, "Because who wants to climb two flights of stairs to their bedroom when they're seventy-eight?"

Others we know have encountered similar situations in their personal lives. After a health crisis, one couple found the luxurious tub for two they slaved over installing had become a specter of a bad slip and safety risks. It's important to think through what your physical reality could be, whatever your long-term plan might be, and it's amazing how many people don't.

Contracts and Regulations

If you are looking into a cross-country move, be aware of new tax tables or local ordinances in the area where you are looking to move. After all, you don't want to experience sticker-shock when you are looking at downsizing or reducing your bills in retirement.

Along the same lines, if you are moving into a retirement community, be sure to look at the fine print. What will happen if you must move into a different situation for long-term care? Will you be penalized? Will you be responsible for replacing your slot in the community? What are all of the fees, and what do they cover?

We have a lot of clients right now who are looking to downsize as they reach their late sixties and seventies. And, while downsizing has a lot of benefits for certain couples as they get older, it also can have some unexpected expenses. For example, the family home they may have paid off, or did not account for, in their expenses because they no longer have a mortgage is added back in if a family must take out a loan on a smaller, but newer, condo or townhome. Also, in these instances, many condos have high HOA/COA fees—in some places as much as $500 or $700 per month—on top of their mortgage payment!

Speaking of mortgages and loans, the banks have made it more difficult for seniors, who are without "normal" sources of employment income, to get qualified for these loans. So, there are certainly some things to consider for families considering a change to their living circumstances or situations later in life.

Inflation

As we write this in 2020, America has experienced a long stretch of low inflation, with average annual inflation not exceeding 4 percent since 1991.[18]

However, inflation isn't a one-time bump; it has a cumulative effect. Even with relatively low inflation over the past few decades, the $20 sneakers you bought your grade-schooler in 1991 will cost $34.02 to buy for your grandchild.[19] What if, in retirement, we hit a stretch like in the late '70s and

---

[18] US Inflation Calculator. January 2020. "Historical Inflation Rates." http://www.usinflationcalculator.com/inflation/historical-inflation-rates/
[19] Ibid.

early '80s when annual inflation rates of 10 percent became the norm? It may be wise to consider some extra padding in your retirement income plan to account for any potential increase in inflation in the future.

Aging

Also, in the expense category, think about longevity. We all hope to age gracefully. However, it's important to face the prospect of aging with a sense of realism.

The elephant in the room for many families is long-term care: No one wants to admit they will likely need it, but the reality is it's estimated that as many as 70 percent of us will.[20] Aging is a significant piece of retirement income planning because you'll want to figure out how to set aside money for your care, either at home or away from it. The more comfortable you get with discussing your wishes and plans with your loved ones, the easier planning for the financial side of it can be.

We discuss health care and potential long-term care costs in more detail elsewhere in this book, but, suffice it to say, nursing home care can be expensive and typically not something you get to choose when you need.

It isn't just the costs of long-term care that pose a concern in living longer. It's also about covering the possible costs of everything else associated with living longer. For instance, if Henry retires from his job as a biochemical engineer at age sixty-five, perhaps he planned to have a very decent income for twenty years, until age eighty-five. But what if he lives until he's ninety-five? That's a whole third—ten years—more of personal income he will need.

---

[20] Moll Law Group. 2019. "The Cost of Long-Term Care." https://www.molllawgroup.com/the-cost-of-long-term-care.html.

Putting It All Together

Whew! So, you have pulled together what you have, and you have a pretty good idea of where you want to be. Now your financial professional and you can go about the work of arranging what assets you *have* to cover what you need—and how you might try to cover any gaps.

Like the proverbial man in the Bible who built his house on a rock, we like to help our clients figure out how to cover their day-to-day living expenses—their needs—with insurance and other guaranteed income sources, like pensions and Social Security.

Our process for helping families and couples determine whether they can retire is by putting together a comprehensive, detailed financial plan, called a "Roadmap to Retirement." This important step helps them figure out exactly where they are currently at and exactly where the next ten or twenty years (and more) will lead them. We do not leave anything to chance, and we always help folks plan for the worst and hope for the best.

Again, you should keep in mind there isn't one single financial vehicle, asset, or source to fill all of your needs, and that's okay. One of the challenges of making a plan for your income in retirement concerns figuring out what products to use. You can release some of that stress when you accept the fact you will need a diverse portfolio—potentially with bonds, stocks, insurance, and other income sources—not just one massive money pile.

One way to help shore up your income gaps is by working with your financial professional and a qualified tax advisor to mitigate your tax exposure. Effective tax planning isn't just about "adding" to your income; especially with retirement, it's less about what you make as it is about what you keep. Paying a lower tax bill keeps more money in your pocket, which is where you want it when it comes to retirement income.

Now you can look at ways to cover your remaining retirement goals. Are there products like long-term care insurance specific to a certain kind of expense you anticipate? Is there a particular asset you want to use for your "play" money—money for trips and gifts for the grandkids? Is there any way you can portion off money for those charitable legacy plans?

Once you have analyzed your income wants, needs, and your realistic assets to cover them, you may have a gap. The masterstroke of a competent financial professional will be to help you figure out how you will cover that gap. Will you need to cut out a round of golf a week? Maybe skip the new car? Or will you need to take more substantial action?

One way to cover an income gap is to consider working longer or even part-time before retirement and even after that magical calendar date. This may not be the best "plan" for you; disabilities, work demands, and physical or emotional limitations can hinder the best-laid plans to continue working. However, if it is physically possible for you, this is one considerable way to help your assets last, for more than one reason.

In fact, about one in five Americans are still working past age sixty-five. This is a record percentage in the past half-century. While some do list their personal finances as a reason for staying on the job, others do so to avoid feeling bored in retirement, among other reasons.[21]

One woman, a physician's assistant, came in and told us she had been saving and preparing, on her own, for retirement. But, when she came to see us, she really had no idea whether the preparations and savings she had accumulated were sufficient—would it be enough? She was pleasantly surprised and pleased to find out she could retire.

These are situations we absolutely love to discover here at our office. We live for when we can make someone's day—and future—so exciting by telling them, after working for all these

---

[21] Associated Press. October 9, 2018. "1 in 5 Americans over 65 are Still Waiting to Retire." https://nypost.com/2018/10/09/1-in-5-americans-over-65-are-still-waiting-to-retire/.

years, they have put themselves in a position to retire comfortably and confidently. Of course, proper planning and keeping that hard-earned money for the next several decades becomes vital for these discoveries to happen. We are proud to help make this possible for clients every day.

When you're retired, you no longer have an employer paying you a steady check. It is up to you to make sure you have saved and planned for the income you need.

CHAPTER 5
Social Security

Social Security is often the foundation piece of retirement income. Backed by the strength of the U.S. Treasury, it provides perhaps the most dependable paycheck you will have in retirement.

From the time you collect your first paycheck at whatever job made you a bonafide taxpayer (Bill particularly remembers his first job at Chatham's Supermarkets on Morang and 7 mile in Detroit) you are paying into the grand old Social Security system. What grew and developed out of the pressures of the Great Depression has become one of the most popular government programs in the country, and, if you pay in the equivalent of ten years or more, you, too, can benefit from the Social Security program.

Now, before we get into the nitty-gritty of Social Security, we'd like to address a current concern: Will Social Security still be there for you when you reach retirement age?

The Future of Social Security

This question is ever-present as headlines trumpet an underfunded Social Security program alongside the flux of baby boomers who are retiring in droves and the comparatively smaller younger generations who are bearing the responsibility of funding the system.

The Social Security Administration itself is a source of this concern as each Social Security statement now bears an asterisk that continues near the end of the summary:

> "*Your estimated benefits are based on current law. Congress has made changes to the law in the past and can do so at any time. The law governing benefit amounts may change because, by 2034, the payroll taxes collected will be enough to pay only about 79 percent of scheduled benefits."

Just a reminder, as if you needed one, that nothing in life is guaranteed.

Before you get too discouraged, though, here are a few thoughts to keep you going:

- Although those who retire after 2034 may only receive 79 cents on the dollar for their scheduled benefits, 79 percent is notably not zero.
- The Social Security Administration has made changes in the distant and near past to protect the fund's solvency, including increasing retirement ages and striking certain filing strategies.
- There are many changes Congress could make, and lawmakers are currently discussing how to fix the system, such as further increasing full retirement age and eligibility.
- One thing no one is seriously discussing? Reneging on current obligations to retirees or the soon-to-retire.

Take heart. The real answer to the question, "Will Social Security be there for me?" is still "yes."

This question is important to consider when you take a look at how we, as a nation, rely on this program. Did you know Social Security benefits replace about 40 percent of a person's original income when they retire?[22] If you ask me, that's a pretty significant piece of your retirement income puzzle.

Another caveat? You may not realize this, but no one can legally "advise" you about your Social Security benefits.

"But, guys," you may be thinking, "Isn't that part of what you do? And what about that nice gentleman at the Social Security Administration office I spoke with on the phone?"

Don't get us wrong. Social Security Administration employees know their stuff. They are trained to know policies and programs, and they are usually pretty quick to tell you what you can and cannot do. But the government specifically says, because Social Security is a benefit you alone have paid into and earned, your Social Security decisions, too, are yours alone.

When it comes to financial professionals, we can't push you in any directions, either, *but*—there's a big but here—working with a well-informed financial professional is still incredibly handy when it comes to your Social Security decisions. Why? Because someone who's worth his or her salt will know what withdrawal strategies might pertain to your specific situation and will ask questions that can help you determine what you are looking for when it comes to your Social Security.

For instance, some people want the highest possible monthly benefit. Others want to start their benefits early, not always because of financial need. We heard about one man who called in to start his Social Security payments the day he qualified, just because he liked to think of it as the government paying back a debt it owed him, and he enjoyed the feeling of receiving a check from Uncle Sam.

Whatever your reasons, questions, or feelings regarding Social Security, the decision is yours alone; but working with a financial professional can help you put your options in perspective by showing you—both with industry knowledge and with proprietary software or planning processes—where your benefits fit into your overall strategy for retirement income.

---

[22] Social Security Administration. "Learn About Social Security Programs." https://www.ssa.gov/planners/retire/r&m6.html

One reason the federal government doesn't allow for "advice" related to Social Security, we suspect, is so no one can profit from giving you advice related to your Social Security benefit—or from providing any clarifications. Again, this is a sign of a good financial professional. Those who are passionate about their work will be knowledgeable about what benefit strategies might be to your advantage and will happily share those possible options with you.

Full Retirement Age

When it comes to Social Security, it seems like many people only think so far as "yes." They don't take the time to understand the various options available. Instead, because it is common knowledge you can begin your benefits at age sixty-two, that's what many of us do. While more people are opting to delay taking benefits, age sixty-two is still firmly the most popular age to start.[23]

What many people fail to understand is, by starting benefits early, they may be leaving a lot of money on the table. You see, the Social Security Administration bases your monthly benefit on two factors: your earnings history and your full retirement age (FRA). From your earnings history, they pull the thirty-five years you made the most money and use a mathematical indexing formula to figure out a monthly average from those years. If you paid into the system for less than thirty-five years, then every year you didn't pay in will be counted as a zero.

Once they have calculated what your monthly earning would be at FRA, the government then calculates what to put on your check based on how close you are to FRA.

---

[23] Elizabeth O'Brien. Money. March 7, 2019. "This is the Age when Most People Claim Social Security—and When Experts Say You Really Should." http://money.com/money/5637694/this-is-the-age-when-most-people-claim-social-security-and-when-experts-say-you-really-should/

Age to Receive Full Social Security Benefits*	
(Called "full retirement age" [FRA] or "normal retirement age.")	
Year of Birth*	FRA
1937 or earlier	65
1938	65 and 2 months
1939	65 and 4 months
1940	65 and 6 months
1941	65 and 8 months
1942	65 and 10 months
1943-1954	66
1955	66 and 2 months
1956	66 and 4 months
1957	66 and 6 months
1958	66 and 8 months
1959	66 and 10 months
1960 and later	67
If you were born on Jan. 1 of any year, you should refer to the previous year. (If you were born on the 1st of the month, we figure your benefit [and your full retirement age] as if your birthday was in the previous month.)	

FRA was originally set at sixty-five, but, as the population aged and lifespans lengthened, the government shifted FRA later and later based on an individual's year of birth. Check out the preceding chart to see when you will reach FRA. [24]

When you attain FRA, you are eligible to receive 100 percent of whatever the Social Security Administration says is your full monthly benefit.

Starting at age sixty-two, for every year before FRA you claim benefits, your monthly check is reduced by 5 percent. Conversely, for every year you delay taking benefits past FRA, your monthly benefit increases by 8 percent (until age seventy—after that, there is no monetary advantage to delaying Social Security benefits). While your circumstances and needs may vary, this is why a lot of financial professionals urge people to at least consider delaying until they reach age seventy.

Why Wait? [25]

Taking benefits early could affect your monthly check by _____.								
62	63	64	65	FRA 66	67	68	69	70
-20%	-15%	-10%	-5%	0	+8%	+16%	+24%	+32%

My Social Security

As long as you are over age thirty, you have probably received a notice from the Social Security Administration telling you to activate something called "My Social Security." This is a handy way to learn more about your particular benefit options, to keep track of what your earnings record looks like, and to calculate the benefits you have accrued over the years.

---

[24] Social Security Administration. "Full Retirement Age." https://www.ssa.gov/planners/retire/retirechart.html
[25] Social Security Administration. April 2019. "Can You Take Your Benefits Before Full Retirement Age?" https://www.ssa.gov/planners/retire/applying2.html

Essentially, My Social Security is an online account you can activate to see what your personal Social Security picture looks like, which you can do at www.ssa.gov/myaccount. This can be extremely helpful when it comes to planning for income in retirement and figuring up the difference between your anticipated income versus anticipated expenses.

My Social Security is also helpful because it's a great way to see if there is a problem. For instance, we have heard of one woman who, through diligently checking her tax records against her Social Security profile, discovered her Social Security check was shortchanging her, based on her earnings history. After taking the discrepancy to the Social Security Administration, they sent her what they owed her in makeup benefits.

COLA

Social Security is a largely guaranteed piece of the retirement puzzle: If you get a statement that says to expect $1,000 a month, you can be sure you will receive $1,000 a month. But there is one variable detail, and that is something called the cost-of-living adjustment, or COLA.

The COLA is an increase in your monthly check meant to address inflation in everyday life. After all, your expenses will likely continue to experience inflation in retirement, but you will no longer have the opportunity for raises, bonuses, or promotions you had when you were working. Instead, Social Security receives an annual cost-of-living increase tied to the Department of Labor's Consumer Price Index for Urban Wage Earners and Clerical Workers, or CPI-W. If the CPI-W measurement shows inflation rose a certain amount for regular goods and services, then Social Security recipients will see that reflected in their COLA.

The COLA averages 4 percent, but in a no- or low-inflation environment, such as in 2010, 2011, and 2016, Social Security recipients will not receive an adjustment. Some view the COLA as a perk, bump, or bonus, but, in reality, it works more like this: Your mom sends you to the store with $2.50 for a gallon of milk. Milk costs exactly $2.50. The next week, you go back with that same amount, but it is now $2.52 for a gallon, so you go back to Mom, and she gives you 2 cents. You aren't bringing home more milk—it just costs more money.

So the COLA is less about "making" more money and more about keeping seniors' purchasing power from eroding when inflation is a big factor, such as in 1975, when it was 8 percent![26] Still, don't let that detract from your enthusiasm about COLAs; after all, what if Mom's solution was: "Here's the same $2.50; try to find pennies from somewhere else to get that milk!"?

Spousal Benefits

We've talked about FRA, but another big Social Security decision involves spousal benefits.

If you or your spouse has a long stretch of zeros in your earnings history—perhaps if one of you stayed home for years, caring for children or sick relatives—you may want to consider filing for spousal benefits instead of filing on your own earnings history. A spousal benefit can be up to 50 percent of the primary wage earner's benefit at full retirement age.

To begin drawing a spousal benefit, you must be at least sixty-two years old, and the primary wage earner must have already filed for his or her benefit. While there are penalties for taking spousal benefits early (you could lose up to 67.5 percent of your check for filing at age sixty-two), you cannot earn credits for delaying past full retirement age.[27]

Like we said, the spousal benefit can be a big deal for those who don't have a very long pay history, but it's important to

---

[26] Social Security Administration. "Cost-Of-Living Adjustment (COLA) Information for 2019." https://www.ssa.gov/cola/

[27] Social Security Administration. "Retirement Planner: Benefits For You As A Spouse." https://www.ssa.gov/planners/retire/applying6.html

weigh your own earned benefits against the option of withdrawing based on a fraction of your spouse's benefits.

To look at how this could play out, let's use a hypothetical example of Mary Jane, who is sixty, and Peter, who is sixty-two.

Let's say Peter's benefit at FRA, in his case sixty-six, would be $1,600. If Peter begins his benefits right now, four years before FRA, his monthly check will be $1,200. If Mary Jane begins taking spousal benefits in two years, at the earliest date possible, her monthly benefits will be reduced by 67.5 percent, to $520 per month (remember, at FRA, the most she can qualify for is half of Peter's FRA benefit).

What if Peter and Mary Jane both wait until FRA? At sixty-six, Peter begins taking his full benefit of $1,600 a month. Two years later, when she reaches age sixty-six, Mary Jane will qualify for $800 a month. By waiting until FRA, the couple's monthly benefit goes from $1,720 to $2,400.

What if Peter delays until age seventy to get his maximum possible benefit? For each year past FRA he delays, his monthly benefits increase by 8 percent. This means, at seventy, he could file for a monthly benefit of $2,112. However, delayed retirement credits do not affect spousal benefits, so as soon as Peter files at seventy, Mary Jane would also file (at age sixty-eight) for her maximum benefit of $800, so their highest possible combined monthly check is $2,912.[28]

When it comes to your Social Security benefits, you obviously will want to consider if a monthly check based on a fraction of your spouse's earnings will be comparable to or larger than your own earnings history.

We've thrown a lot of numbers at you to consider, like your FRA based on your year of birth, as well as COLA and spousal benefits (and we haven't even gotten to taxes!), but here's another date to think about: Jan. 2, 1954. What's important about that, you ask? For those born on or after that date, you

---

[28] Office of the Chief Actuary. Social Security Administration. "Social Security Benefits: Benefits for Spouses."
https://www.ssa.gov/OACT/quickcalc/spouse.html#calculator

can only make the choice to withdraw your benefits one way, one time. That means you will have to pick whether to take a spousal benefit or use your own earnings history, and whichever one you choose will be the check you get every month for the duration of your retirement. However, if you were born **before** Jan. 2, 1954, read on.

If you were born before Jan. 2, 1954, you are eligible to change your benefit withdrawal strategy *even after you have begun withdrawals*. This means you could begin taking a spousal benefit at sixty-two or at FRA while allowing the benefits based on your own earnings history to accrue.[29]

Let's look back to Mary Jane and Peter to see how this could theoretically work. We know, if they both file at FRA, Mary Jane will receive $800 a month on top of Peter's $1,600 benefit when she files. But, what if her own earned credit at FRA was $700? In four years, when Mary Jane turns seventy, the monthly benefit based on her personal earnings will have grown from $700 to $924. At seventy, she could file to trade up her $800 monthly spousal benefit for a $924 monthly check. Remember, this only works for Mary Jane if she was born before January 2, 1954.

Divorced Spouses

There are a few considerations for those of us who have gone through a divorce. If you 1) were married for ten years or more *and* 2) have since been divorced for at least two years *and* 3) are unmarried *and* 4) your ex-spouse qualifies to begin Social Security, you qualify for a spousal benefit based on your ex-husband or ex-wife's earnings history at FRA. A divorced spousal benefit is different from the married spousal benefit in

---

[29] Social Security Administration. "Retirement Planner: Benefits For Your Spouse." https://www.ssa.gov/planners/retire/applying6.html

one way: You don't have to wait for your ex-spouse to file before you can file yourself.[30]

For instance, Charles and Moira were married for fifteen years before their divorce, when he was thirty-six and she was forty. Moira has been remarried for twenty years, and, although Charles briefly remarried, his second marriage ended after a few years. Charles' benefits are largely calculated based on his many years of volunteering in schools, meaning his personal monthly benefit is close to zero.

Although Moira has deferred her retirement, opting to delay benefits until she is seventy, Charles can begin taking benefits calculated off of Moira's work history at FRA as early as age sixty-two. However, he will also have the option of waiting until FRA to collect the maximum, 50 percent, of Moira's earned monthly benefit at her FRA.

Widowed Spouses

If your marriage ended with the death of your spouse, you might claim a benefit for your spouse's earned income as his or her widow/widower, called a survivor's benefit. Unlike a spousal benefit or divorced benefits, if your husband or wife dies, you are allowed to claim his or her full benefit. Also, unlike spousal benefits, if you need to, you can begin taking income when you turn sixty. However, as with other benefit options, your monthly check will be permanently reduced for withdrawing benefits before FRA.

If your spouse began taking benefits before he or she died, you can't delay withdrawing your survivor's benefits to get delayed credits; the Social Security Administration says you can

---

[30] Social Security Administration. "Retirement Planner: If You Are Divorced." https://www.ssa.gov/planners/retire/divspouse.html

only get as much from a survivor's benefit as what your deceased spouse might have gotten, had he or she lived.[31]

Taxes, Taxes, Taxes

With Social Security, as with everything, it is important to consider taxes. It may be surprising, but your Social Security benefits are not tax-free. Despite having been taxed to accrue those benefits in the first place, you may have to pay Uncle Sam income taxes on up to 85 percent of your Social Security.

The Social Security Administration figures these taxes using what they call "the provisional income formula." Your provisional income formula differs from the adjusted gross income you use for your regular income taxes. Instead, to find out how much of your Social Security benefit is taxable, the Social Security Administration calculates it this way:

Provisional Income = Adjusted Gross Income + Nontaxable Interest + ½ of Social Security

See that piece about nontaxable interest? That generally means interest from government bonds and notes. It surprises many people that, although you may not pay taxes on those assets, their income will count against you when it comes to Social Security taxation.

Once you have figured out your provisional income (also called "combined income"), you can use the following chart to figure out your Social Security taxes.[32]

---

[31] Social Security Administration. "Benefits Planner: Receiving Survivors Benefits Early." https://www.ssa.gov/planners/survivors/survivorchartred.html

[32] Social Security Administration. "Benefits Planner: Income Taxes and Your Social Security Benefit." https://www.ssa.gov/planners/taxes.html

Taxes on Social Security		
Provisional Income = Adjusted Gross Income + Nontaxable Interest + ½ of Social Security		
If you are ___ and your provisional income is ___, then...		Uncle Sam will tax ___ of your Social Security
Single	Married, filing jointly	
Less than $25,000	Less than $32,000	0%
$25,000 to $34,000	$32,000 to $44,000	Up to 50%
More than $34,000	More than $44,000	Up to 85%

This is one more reason it may benefit you to work with a financial professional: He or she can take a look at your entire picture to make your overall retirement plan as tax-efficient as possible—including your Social Security benefit.

One strategy we use to help reposition a couple's Social Security income and benefit to make it more tax-efficient is to determine at what age it would be most appropriate for the client to start taking their Social Security Income (SSI).

For some families, it is better to wait because, by waiting until Full Retirement Age, not only do they receive more income, but it also allows them to keep working in a higher paying position for longer. However, if a client is retired or has retired by age sixty-two, then the consideration might be different. Now, the question will depend on when the client needs the income to begin, how much they will need, and from what source it will need to come.

Working and Social Security: The Earnings Test

If you haven't reached FRA, but you started your Social Security benefits and are still working, things get a little hairy.

Because you have started Social Security payments, the Social Security Administration will pay out your benefits (docked, of course, for what you could have gotten if you had waited to file until your FRA). Yet, because you are working, the organization must also withhold from your check to add to your benefits . . . which you are already collecting. See how this complicates matters?

To straighten the situation, the government has what is called "the earnings test." For 2020, you can earn up to $18,240 without it affecting your Social Security check. But, for every $2 you earn past that amount, the Social Security Administration will withhold $1. The earnings test loosens in the year of your FRA; if you are reaching FRA in 2020, you can earn up to $48,600 before you run into the earnings test, and the government only withholds $1 for every $3 past that amount.

In the month you will reach FRA, you are no longer subject to any earnings withholding. For instance, if you are still working and will turn sixty-six on December 28, 2020, you would only have to worry about the earnings test until December, and then you can ignore it entirely.

Keep in mind, the money the government withholds from your Social Security benefits while you are working before FRA will be tacked back onto your benefits check after FRA.[33]

We can assist clients by showing them various ways to take Social Security income, based on their Roadmap to Retirement. Again, we help take any guesswork out of it and show how

---

[33] Social Security Administration. "Exempt Amounts Under the Earnings Test." https://www.ssa.gov/oact/cola/rtea.html

clients could receive more money over time, based on their individual plan.

CHAPTER 6

401(k)s & IRAs

Have you heard? Today's retirement is not your dad's retirement. You see, back in the day, it was pretty common to work for one company for the vast majority of your career and then retire with a gold watch and a pension.

The gold watch was a symbol of the quality time you had put in at that company, but the pension was more than a symbol. Instead, it was a guarantee—as solid as your employer—that they would repay your hard work with a certain amount of income in your old age. Did you see the caveat there? Your pension's guarantee was *as solid as your employer*. The problem was, what if your employer went under?

Companies that failed couldn't pay their retired employees' pensions, leading to financial challenges for many. Beginning in 1974 with Congress' passage of the Employee Retirement Income Security Act, federal legislation and regulations aimed at protecting retirees were everywhere. One piece of legislation included a relatively obscure section of the Internal Revenue Code, added in 1978. Section 401(k), to be specific.

IRC section 401, subsection k, created tax advantages for employer-sponsored financial products, even if the main contributor was the employee him or herself. Over the years, more employers took note, beginning an age of transition away from pensions and toward 401(k) plans. A 401(k) is a retirement account with certain tax benefits and restrictions on the investments or other financial products inside of it.

Essentially, 401(k)s and their individual retirement account (IRA) counterparts are "wrappers" that provide tax benefits around assets; typically, the assets that compose IRAs and 401(k)s are mutual funds, stock and bond mixes, and money market accounts. However, IRA and 401(k) contents are becoming more diverse these days, with some companies offering different kinds of annuity options within their plans.

Where pensions are defined-*benefit* plans, 401(k)s and IRAs are defined-*contribution* plans. The one-word change outlines the basic difference. Pensions spell out what you can expect to receive from the plan but not necessarily how much money it will take to fund those benefits. With 401(k)s, an employer sets a standard for how much they will contribute (if any), and you can be certain of what you are contributing. Still, there is no outline for what you can expect to receive in return for those contributions.

Modern employment looks very different these days. A 2018 survey by the Bureau of Labor Statistics determined U.S. workers stayed with their employers a median of about four years. Workers ages fifty-five to sixty-four had a little more staying power and were most likely to stay with their employer for about ten years.[34] Additionally, in 1979, when those employees would have been hitting their strides, career-wise, 38 percent of workers had pensions. But 401(k)s are rising in number, with about 55 million American workers enrolled in a plan.[35]

A far cry from a pension and gold watch, wouldn't you say?

When folks are planning for retirement without a pension, it becomes even more important for them to know exactly where their income will come from during their retirement years. Other than Social Security income, there is not a default safety-

---

[34] Bureau of Labor Statistics. September 20, 2018. "Employee Tenure Summary." https://www.bls.gov/news.release/tenure.nr0.htm

[35] Investment Company Institute. December 31, 2018. "Frequently Asked Questions about 401(k) Plan Research." https://www.ici.org/policy/retirement/plan/401k/faqs_401k

net or income source to fall back on, so planning is even more crucial. Where is your income going to come from? Your investments? Your savings? It has to be determined ahead of time.

Entering retirement without a pension requires even more precise planning with your advisor. But with a pension, a family has two sources of income—their pension and Social Security—and we use those assets to determine how their investments fit into their retirement income picture.

If there is anything to learn from this paradigm shift, it's that you have to look out for you. Whether you have worked for a company for two years or twenty, you are still the one who has to look out for your own best interests. That holds doubly true when it comes to preparing for retirement. If you are one of the lucky ones who still has a pension, good for you. But for the rest of us, it is likely a 401(k)—or possibly one of its nonprofit- or government-sector counterparts, a 403(b) or 457 plan—is one of your biggest assets for retirement.

Some employers offer incentives to contribute to their company plans, like a company match. On that subject, we have one thing to say: *do it!* Nothing in life is free, as they say, but a company match on your retirement funds is about as close to free money as we think it gets. If you can make the minimum to qualify for your company's match at all, go for it.

Now, it's likely, during our working years, we mostly "set and forget" our 401(k) funding. Because it is tax-advantaged, your employer is taking money from your paycheck—before taxes—and putting it into your plan for you. Maybe you got to pick a selection of investments, or maybe your company only offers one choice of investment in your 401(k). But, when you are ready to retire or move jobs, you have choices to make requiring a little more thought and care.

When you are ready to part ways with your job, you have a few options:

- Leave the money where it is

- Take the cash (and pay income taxes and perhaps a 10 percent additional federal tax if you are younger than age fifty-nine-and-one-half)
- Transfer the money to another employer plan (if the new plan allows)
- Roll the money over into a self-directed IRA

Now, these are just general options. You will have to decide, with the help of a financial professional registered to provide investment advice, what's right for you. For instance, 401(k)s are typically pretty closely tied to the companies offering them, so when changing jobs, it may not always be possible to transfer a 401(k) to another 401(k). Leaving the money where it is may also be out of the question—some companies have direct cash payout or rollover policies once someone is no longer employed.

Remember what we said earlier about how we change jobs more often these days? That means you likely have a 401(k) with your current company, but you may also have a string of IRAs trailing you from other jobs.

When it comes to your retirement income, it's important to be able to pull together *all* of your assets, so you can examine what you have and where, and then decide what you will do with it.

Tax-Qualified, Tax-Preferred, Tax-Deferred . . . Still TAXED

Financial media often cite IRAs and 401(k)s for their tax benefits. After all, with traditional plans, you put your money in, pre-tax, and it hopefully grows for years, even decades, untaxed. That's why these accounts are called "tax-qualified" or "tax-deferred" assets. They aren't *tax-free*! Rarely does Uncle Sam allow business to continue without receiving his piece of the pie, and your retirement assets are no different. If you didn't pay taxes on the front end, you will pay taxes on the money you withdraw from these accounts in retirement. Don't get us wrong: This isn't an inherently bad thing, nor is it a good thing; it's just the way it is. It's important to understand, though, for the sake of planning ahead.

In retirement, many people assume they will be in a lower tax bracket. Are you planning to pare down your lifestyle in retirement? Perhaps you are, and perhaps you will have substantially less income in retirement. But many of our clients tell us they want to live life more or less the same as they always have. The money they would previously have spent on business attire or gas for their commute they now want to spend on hobbies and grandchildren. That's all fine, and, for many of them, it is doable, but does it put them in a lower tax bracket? No.

Because of their special tax status, IRAs, 401(k)s, and their alternatives have a few limitations you should understand. For one thing, the IRS sets limits on your contributions to these retirement accounts. If you are contributing to a 401(k) or an equivalent nonprofit or government plan, your annual contribution limit is $19,500 (as of 2020). If you are fifty or older, the IRS allows additional contributions, called "catch-up contributions," of up to $6,500 on top of the regular limit of $19,500. For an IRA, the limit is $6,000, with a catch-up limit of an additional $1,000. [36]

Because their tax advantages come from their intended use as retirement income, withdrawing funds from these accounts before you turn fifty-nine-and-one-half can carry stiff penalties. In addition to fees your investment management company might charge, you will have to pay income tax *and* a 10 percent federal tax penalty.

---

[36] Troy Segal. Investopedia. January 17, 2020. "What Are the Roth 401(k) Contribution Limits."
https://www.investopedia.com/ask/answers/102714/what-are-roth-401k-contibution-limits.asp

Now, there are a few exceptions to the fifty-nine-and-one-half rule:[37]

Exceptions to the 59½ Rule	
Exception	**Applies to IRA or 401(k)**
Death of account holder	Both
Total, permanent disability of account holder	Both
First-time homebuyer (up to $10,000)	IRA
Certain higher education expenses	IRA
Unreimbursed medical expenses greater than 10% of income	Both
Separation from employer service after age 55	401(k)

Other than these exceptions, though, the fifty-nine-and-one-half rule for retirement accounts is incredibly important to remember, especially when you're young. Many millennials we see in our practice come in and, while they may be socking money away in their workplace retirement plan, it's often the *only* place they are saving. This could be problematic later because of the fifty-nine-and-one-half rule. What if you have an emergency? It is important to fund your retirement, but you

---

[37] IRS. October 29, 2019. "Retirement Topics: Exceptions to Tax on Early Distributions." https://www.irs.gov/retirement-plans/plan-participant-employee/retirement-topics-tax-on-early-distributions

need to have access to emergency funds. This can help you avoid breaking into your retirement accounts and incurring taxes and penalties as a result of the fifty-nine-and-one-half rule.

RMDs

Remember how we talked about the 401(k) or IRA being a "tax wrapper" for your funds? Well, eventually, Uncle Sam will want a bite of that candy bar. So, beginning at age seventy-two, the government requires you withdraw a portion of your account, which the IRS calculates based on the size of your account and your estimated lifespan. This required minimum distribution, or RMD, is the government's insurance it will collect some taxes, at some point, from your earnings. Because you didn't pay taxes on the front end, you will now pay income taxes on whatever you withdraw, including your RMDs. Also, let us just remind you not to play chicken with the U.S. government; if you don't take your RMDs starting at age seventy-two, you will have to write a check to the IRS for 50 *percent* of the amount of your missed RMDs.

If you don't need income from your retirement accounts, RMDs can seem like more of a tax burden than an income boon. While some people prefer to reinvest their RMDs, this comes with the possibility of additional taxation: You'll pay income taxes on your RMDs and then capital gains taxes on the growth of your investments. If you are legacy minded, there are other ways to use RMDs, many of which have tax benefits.

Permanent Life Insurance
One way to turn those pesky RMDs into a legacy is through permanent life insurance. If properly structured, these products avoid taxation and can pass on a sizeable death benefit to your beneficiaries, tax-free, as part of your general legacy plan.

ILIT

Another way to use RMDs toward your legacy is to work with an estate planning attorney to create an irrevocable life insurance trust (ILIT). This is basically a permanent life insurance policy within a trust. Because the trust is irrevocable, you would relinquish control of it, but, unlike just a permanent life insurance policy, your death benefit won't count toward your taxable estate.

Annuities

Because annuities can be tax-deferred, using your RMDs to purchase an annuity contract can be one way to further delay taxation while guaranteeing your income payments (either to you or your loved ones) later.

Qualified Charitable Distributions

If you are charity-minded, you may use your RMDs toward a charitable organization instead of using them for income. You must do this directly from your retirement account (you can't take the RMD check and *then* pay the charity) for your withdrawals to be qualified charitable distributions (QCDs), but this is one way of realizing some of the benefits of a charitable legacy during your own lifetime. You will not need to pay taxes on your QCDs, and they won't count toward your annual charitable tax deduction limit, plus you'll be able to see how the organization you are supporting uses your donations. It is advisable to consult a financial professional on how to correctly make a QCD, particularly since the SECURE Act of 2019 has implemented a few minor regulations on this point.[38]

---

[38] Bob Carlson. Forbes. January 28, 2020. "More Questions And Answers About The SECURE Act."
https://www.forbes.com/sites/bobcarlson/2020/01/28/more-questions-and-answers-about-the-secure-act/#113d49564869

Roth

Since the Taxpayer Relief Act of 1997, there has been a different kind of retirement account available to the public: the Roth. Roth IRAs and Roth 401(k)s each differ from their traditional counterparts in one big way: You pay your taxes on the front end. This means, once your post-tax money is in the Roth account, as long as you follow the rules and limitations of that account (the account has been open for at least five years and you take withdrawals after age fifty-nine-and-one-half), your distributions are truly tax-free. You won't pay income tax when you take withdrawals, so, in turn, you don't have to worry about RMDs. However, Roth accounts have the same limitations as traditional 401(k)s and IRAs when it comes to withdrawing money before age fifty-nine-and-one-half.

One of our common strategies for helping clients mitigate the tax consequences of RMDs is to look at the possibility of converting some of their IRA money to a Roth IRA before they reach the age of seventy-two and paying the taxes due at the time of conversion, at today's tax rates. This is typically more appropriate if their income tax bracket is low during the year in question. For example, a very high earner may not find it as advantageous to do a Roth IRA conversion as a lower earner might find it. This conversion would lower the amount of RMDs withdrawn when the person does reach age seventy-two, when the distribution is then required.

Another possibility would be to take withdrawals or income out of their IRAs before reaching seventy-two (and after age fifty-nine-and-one-half), to lower the total amount of RMDs due, while utilizing money the client would have used anyway for normal expenses.

A Roth conversion is a taxable event and may have several tax related consequences. Be sure to consult with a qualified tax advisor before making any decisions regarding your IRA.

Taking Charge

As mentioned earlier, the 401(k) and IRA have largely replaced pensions, but they aren't an equal trade.

Pensions are employer-funded; the money feeding them is money that wouldn't ever show up on your pay stub. Because 401(k)s are self-funded, you have to actively and consciously save. This distinction has made a difference when it comes to funding retirement. According to one NerdWallet article, the average 401(k) balance for a person age sixty to sixty-nine is $198,600, but the median likely tells the full story. The median 401(k) balance for a person age sixty to sixty-nine is $63,000. The article also cites the general suggestion to aim, by age thirty, to have saved up an amount equal to 50 percent to 100 percent of your annual salary.[39] For some thirty-year-olds, saving half an annual salary by age thirty is more than some sixty-to-sixty-nine-year-olds have saved for their entire lives.

There can be many reasons people underfund their retirement plans, like being overwhelmed by the investment choices or taking withdrawals from IRAs when they leave an employer, but we believe the reason at the top of the list is this: People simply aren't participating to begin with.

So, no matter where you're saving, the most important retirement income decision you can make is to sock away your money somewhere in the first place.

---

[39] Arielle O'Shea. Nerd Wallet. January 24, 2019. "The Average 401(k) Balance by Age." https://www.nerdwallet.com/article/investing/the-average-401k-balance-by-age

CHAPTER 7
Annuities

In our practice, we offer our clients a variety of insurance products—from securities to insurance—all designed to help them reach their financial goals. You may be wondering: Why single out a single product in this book?

Well, while most of our clients have a pretty good understanding of business and finance, we sometimes find those who have the impression there must be magic involved. Like turning straw into gold, a harp and a goose that lays golden eggs, or Jack and the Beanstalk going from a cow to a bean to a sack of gold, some people assume there is a magic finance wand we can wave to change years' worth of savings into a strategy for retirement income.

Yet, finances aren't magic; it takes lots of hard work and, typically, several financial products and strategies to pull together a complete retirement plan. Of all the financial products we work with, it seems people find none more mysterious than annuities. And, if we may say, even some of those who recognize the word "annuity" have a limited understanding of the product. So, in the interest of demystifying annuities, let us tell you a little about what an annuity is.

Generally speaking, insurance is a financial hedge against risk. Car owners buy auto insurance to protect their finances in case they injure someone or someone injures them. Homeowners have house insurance to protect their finances in case of a fire, flood, or another disaster. People also have life insurance to protect their finances in case of untimely death. Almost juxtaposed to life insurance, people have annuities in case of a long life; by providing consistent and reliable income payments, annuities can help with financial protection.

The basic premise of an annuity is you, the annuitant, pay an insurance company some amount in exchange for their contractual guarantee they will pay you income for a certain period of time. How that company pays you, for how long, and how much they offer are determined by the annuity contract you enter into with the insurance company.

How You Get Paid

There are two ways for an annuity contract to provide income: The first is through what is called annuitization, and the second is through the use of income riders. We'll get into income riders in a bit, but let's talk about annuitization. That nice, long word is, in our opinion, one reason annuities have a reputation for mystery and misinformation.

Annuitization

When someone "annuitizes" a contract, it is the point where he or she turns on the income stream. Once a contract has been annuitized, there is no going back. With annuities, if the policyholder lives longer than the insurance company planned, the insurance company is still obligated to pay him or her, even if the payments end up being way more than the contract's actual value. If, however, the policyholder dies an untimely death, depending on the contract type, the insurance company may keep anything left of the money that funded the annuity—nothing would be paid out to the contract holder's survivors. You see where that could make some people balk?

At a high level, here's how it looks from the insurance company's side: Numerous people will buy annuities throughout the years and begin collecting income. Some will live longer and collect more payments than others. Some may break even and receive back all that they put in, and some may pass away before receiving their full value. The company prices the annuities with this information in mind. In addition, insurance companies invest the premiums they receive from annuity holders, and use their earnings to help pay benefits.

Now, we show you this to help explain the original concept of annuitization and how it works, from the perspectives of both an insurer and a contract holder. Modern annuities have so many bells and whistles the picture we just described seems too simplified to do them justice, but it's important to at least have a basic concept of annuitization.

Riders

Speaking of bells and whistles, let's talk about riders. Modern annuities have a lot of different options these days, many in the form of riders you can add to your contract for a fee—usually about 1 percent of the contract value per year. Each rider has its particularities, and the types of riders available will vary by the type of annuity contract purchased, but we'll just briefly outline some of these little extras:

- Lifetime income rider: Contract guarantees you an enhanced income for life
- Death benefit rider: Contract pays an enhanced death benefit to your beneficiaries even if you have annuitized
- Return of premium rider: Guarantees you (or your beneficiaries) will at least receive back the premium value of the annuity
- Long-term care rider: Provides a certain amount, sometimes as much as twice the principal value of the contract, to help pay for long-term care if the contract holder is moved to a nursing home or assisted living situation. These riders usually pay benefits for a specified amount of time, such as three to five years.

This isn't an extensive look, and usually the riders have fancier names based on the issuing company, like "Lorem Ipsum Insurance Company Income Preferred Bonus Fixed Index Annuity rider," but we just wanted to show you what some of the general options are in layman's terms.

Types of Annuities

Annuities break down into four basic types: immediate, variable, fixed, and fixed index.

Immediate

Immediate annuities are not terribly popular because they primarily rely on annuitization to provide income—you give the insurance company a lump sum upfront, and your payments begin immediately. Once you begin receiving income payments, the transaction is irreversible, and you no longer have access to your money in a lump sum. When you die, any remaining contract value is typically forfeited to the insurance company.

All other annuity contract types are "deferred" contracts, meaning you fund your policy as a lump sum or over a period of years and you give it the opportunity to grow over time—sometimes years, sometimes decades.

Variable

A variable annuity is an insurance contract as well as an investment. It's sold by insurance companies, but only through someone who is registered to sell investment products. With a variable annuity contract, the insurance company pools the money it receives from annuity holders and invests in investment options called sub-accounts, which in turn invest in the market. This makes it a bit different from the other annuity contract types because it is the only annuity contract in which your money is subject to losses as a result of market declines. Your contract value has a greater opportunity to grow, but it also stands to lose. Additionally, your contract's value will be subject to the underlying investment's fees and limitations—including capital gains taxes, management fees, etc. Once it is time for you to receive income from the contract, the insurance company will pay you a certain income, locked in at whatever your contract's value was.

Variable annuities are, in our opinion, generally not the best vehicle available for use by consumers who are near or in retirement and need reliable income, and this is why we do not offer them. Variable annuities often come with higher fees than other products, usually in the range of 2 to 4 percent, and their built-in product features (such as a lifetime income) can usually be found in other annuity products without the added investment fees. Discussed below, fixed and fixed index annuities are, in our opinion, often better choices for preserving principal and lifetime income possibilities.

Fixed

A traditional fixed annuity is pretty straightforward. You purchase a contract with a guaranteed interest rate and, when you are ready, the insurance company will make regular income payments to you at whatever payout rate your contract guarantees. Those payments will continue for the rest of your life and, if you choose, for the remainder of your spouse's life.

Fixed annuities don't have much in the way of significant upside potential, but many people like them for their guarantees (after all, if your Aunt May lives to be ninety-five, knowing she has an income check later in life can be her mental and financial safety net), as well as for their predictability. Unlike variable annuities, which are subject to market risk and might be up one year and down the next, you can pretty well calculate the value of your fixed annuity over your lifetime.

Fixed Index

To recap, variable annuities take on more risk to offer more possibilities to grow. Fixed annuities have less potential growth, but they protect your principal. In the last couple of decades, many insurance companies have retooled their product line to offer fixed index annuities, which are sort of midway between variable and fixed annuities on the risk/reward spectrum. Fixed index annuities offer greater growth potential than traditional fixed annuities but less than variable annuities. Like traditional fixed annuities, however, fixed index annuities are protected from downside market losses.

Fixed index annuities tie your potential growth to external market indexes, meaning that instead of your contract value growing at a set interest rate like a traditional fixed annuity, it has the potential to grow within a range. Your contract value is credited interest based on the performance of an external market index like the S&P 500 without ever being invested in the market. You don't invest in the S&P 500 directly, but the insurance company will credit your annuity contract based on the S&P 500's gains, up to a cap.

For instance, if your contract caps your interest at 5 percent, then, in a year the S&P 500 gains 3 percent as of your contract anniversary, your annuity value increases 3 percent. If the S&P 500 gains 35 percent, your annuity value gets a 5 percent bump. But, since your money isn't actually invested in the market with a fixed index annuity, if the market nosedives (2000, 2008, and 2020 anyone?), you won't see any increase in your contract value. Conversely, there will also be no decrease in your contract value (other than optional rider costs, if any)—no matter how badly the market performed, you won't lose any of the interest you were credited in previous years.

So, what if the S&P 500 shows a market loss of 30 percent? Your contract value isn't going anywhere. For those who are more interested in protection than growth potential, fixed index annuities can be an attractive option because, when the stock market has a long period of positive performance, a fixed index annuity might enjoy a conservative gain in its value that usually has more upside potential than just offsetting the effects of inflation. And, during stretches when the stock market is erratic and stock values across the board take significant losses? Fixed index annuities won't lose anything from the stock market volatility.

FIAs provide a certain amount of income for the lives of the owner, and many even offer a death benefit for the family. We often recommend FIAs, along with bonds, stocks, mutual funds, and cash, to wholly round-out a client's investment profile where appropriate.

Other Things to Know About Annuities

We just talked about the four different kinds of annuity contracts available, but all of them have some commonalities as annuities.

For all annuities, the contractual guarantees are only as strong as the insurance company that sells the product, which makes it important to thoroughly check the credit ratings of any company whose products you are considering.

Annuities are tax-deferred, meaning you don't have to pay taxes upfront or on interest earnings as the contract value grows. Instead, you will pay ordinary income taxes on your withdrawals. These are meant to be long-term products, so, similar to other tax-deferred or tax-advantaged products, if you begin taking withdrawals from your contract before age fifty-nine-and-one-half, you may have to pay a 10 percent federal tax penalty. Also, while annuities are generally considered illiquid, most contracts allow you to withdraw up to 10 percent of your contract value every year. Withdraw any more, however, and you could incur additional surrender penalties.

Keep in mind, your withdrawals will deplete the accumulated cash value, death benefit, and, possibly, the rider values of your contract.

Annuities, especially FIAs, are an important part of our practice, and they are something often discussed during our meetings with families when it makes sense for their situation. Families can use annuities as a source of guaranteed income for the rest of their lives—much like the pensions we discussed above. However, unlike in a pension, the money can be left to your spouse *and* to children or any other beneficiary you wish to designate.

Annuities aren't for everyone, but it's important to understand them before saying "yea" or "nay" on whether they fit into your plan; otherwise, you're not operating with complete information, wouldn't you agree? Regardless, you should talk to a financial professional who can help you understand annuities, help you dissect your particular financial needs, and help show you whether or not an annuity is appropriate for your retirement income plan.

CHAPTER 8

Estate & Legacy

In our practice, we devote a significant portion of our time to estate matters. After all, we are financial professionals, and what part of the "estate" isn't affected by money matters?

We included this chapter because we have seen many people do estate planning wrong. Clients, or clients' families, have come in after experiencing a death in the family and have found themselves in the middle of probate, high taxes, or a discovery of something unforeseen (often long-term care) draining the estate.

Alternately, we have seen people do it right: clients or families who visit our office to talk about legacies and how to make them last and adult children who have room to grieve without an added burden of unintended costs, without stress from a family ruptured because of inadequate planning.

We'll share some of these stories here. However, we're not going to give you specific advice, since everyone's situation is unique. We only want to give you some things to think about and to underscore the importance of planning ahead.

As many people know, we are very fortunate to have one of the authors of this book, Aaron W. Saoud, in our office. He is an attorney as well as an advisor, so he is able to help with many items and issues an office without an attorney wouldn't be able to help with.

You Can't Take It With You

When it comes to legacy and estate planning, the most important thing is to *do it*. We have heard people from clients to celebrities (rap artist Snoop Dogg comes to mind) say they aren't interested in what happens to their assets when they die because they'll be dead. That's certainly one way to look at it. But we think that's a very selfish way to go about things—we all have people and causes we care about, not to mention those who care about us. Even if the people we love don't *need* what we leave behind, they can still be fined or legally tied up in the probate process or burial costs if we don't plan for those. And that's not even considering what happens if you become incapacitated at some point while you are still alive. Having a plan in place can greatly reduce the stress of those responsibilities on your loved ones; it's just a loving thing to do.

We encourage our clients to use life insurance along with proper estate planning when it's appropriate, as both can be very useful to fully realize their legacy wishes. Remember, properly funded life insurance can be a guaranteed source of tax-deferred money for the beneficiary.

Documents

There are a few documents that lay the groundwork of legacy planning. You've probably heard of all or most of them, but we'd like to review what they are and how people commonly use them. These are all things you should talk about with an estate planning attorney to establish your legacy.

Powers of Attorney

A power of attorney, or POA, is a document giving someone the authority to act on your behalf and in your best interests. These come in handy in situations where you cannot be present (think a vacation where you get stuck in Canada) or, for durable powers of attorney, even when you are incapacitated (think in a coma or coping with dementia).

It is important to have powers of attorney in place and to appoint someone you trust to act on your behalf in these matters. Have you ever heard of someone who was incapacitated after a car accident, whether from head trauma or being in a coma for weeks—sometimes months? Do you think their bills stopped coming due during that time? We like our phone company and our bank, but neither one is about to put a moratorium on sending us bills, particularly not for an extended and interminable period. A power of attorney would have the authority to make sure your mortgage gets paid or your cable gets canceled while you are unable.

You can have multiple POAs and require them to act jointly.

What this looks like: Do you think two heads are better than one? One man, Chris, significantly relied on his two sons' opinions for both his business and personal matters. He appointed both sons as joint POA, requiring both their signoffs for his medical and financial matters.

You can have multiple POAs who can act independently.

What this looks like: Irene had three children with whom she routinely stayed. They lived in different areas of the country, which she thought was an advantage; one month she might be hiking out West, the next she could enjoy the newest off-Broadway production, and the next she could soak up some Southern sun. She named her three children as independently authorized POAs, so, if something happened, no matter where she was, the child closest could step in to act on her behalf.

You can have POAs who have different responsibilities.

What this looks like: Although Luke's friend Claire, a nurse, was his go-to and POA for health-related issues, financial matters usually made her nervous, so he appointed his good neighbor, Matt, as his POA in all of his financial and legal matters.

In addition to POAs, it may be helpful to have an advance medical directive. This is a document in which you have pre-decided what choices you would make about different health scenarios. An advance medical directive can help ease the burden for your medical POA and loved ones, particularly when it comes to end-of-life care.

We really think POAs are so important, and you don't have to look far to realize their significance. You may remember the Terri Schiavo case and how her situation (a lack of a health care power of attorney) had such devistating effects on her family, even becoming national news. Trusting someone to have the responsibility of caring for you or your assets if the time ever comes may seem like a tough task, but it is something you should get done sooner rather than later—because you just never know what the future holds.

Wills

Perhaps the most basic document of legacy planning, a will is a legal document wherein you outline your wishes for your estate. When it comes to your estate after your death, having a will is the foundation of your legacy. Without one, your loved ones are left behind, guessing what you would have wanted, and the court will likely split your assets according to whatever the state's defaults are. Maybe that's exactly what you wanted, as far as anyone knows, right? Because even if you told your nephew he could have your car he's been driving, if it's not in writing, it still might go to the brother, sister, son, or daughter to whom you aren't talking.

However, it may not be enough just to have a will. Even with a will, your assets will be subject to probate. Probate is what we call the state's process for determining a will's validity. A judge will go through your will to question if it conflicts with state law, if it is the most up-to-date document, and if you were mentally competent at the time it was in order, etc. For some, this is a quick, easily-resolved process. For others, particularly if someone steps forward to contest the will, it may take years to settle, all the while subjecting the assets to court costs and attorney's fees.

One other undesirable piece of the probate process is that it is a public process. That means anyone can go to the courthouse, ask for copies of the case, and discover your assets, as well as who is slated to receive what and who is disputing.

As an attorney, Aaron has seen and dealt with the probate process many times, and many of our clients have personal experiences dealing with a public probate process. Just look at the somewhat recent case of Aretha Franklin and her passing without an estate plan in order to see how quickly it can become public news—and a colossal mess—if not planned well.

It's also important to remember beneficiary lines trump wills. So, that large life insurance policy? What if, when you bought it fifteen years ago, you wrote your ex-husband's name on the beneficiary line? Even if you stipulate otherwise in your will, the company holding your policy will pay out to your ex-spouse. Or, how about the thousands of dollars in your IRA you dedicated to "children" thirty years ago, but one of your children was killed in a car accident, leaving his wife and two toddlers behind? That IRA is going to transfer to your remaining children, with nothing for your daughter-in-law and grandchildren.

That may paint a grim portrait, but we can't underscore enough the importance of working with a skilled estate planning attorney to keep your will and beneficiary lines up to date, for the sake of your loved ones, as your life changes.

We have one client whose mom thought she had put everything in order to avoid a mess in passing off her assets upon her death. When he came in to see us, he began telling us about how family members—including long-lost realtives!—were coming out of the woodwork to try and make a claim on his parents' estate. Unfortunately, he really experienced how nasty members of his family could be throughout the whole situation. It is sad, but true, how people can show their true colors when it comes to being left (or left out of) a family's inheritance.

Trusts

Another piece of legacy planning to consider is the trust. A trust is set up through an attorney and allows a third party, or trustee, to hold your assets and determine how they will pass to your beneficiaries. Many people are skeptical of trusts because they assume trusts are only appropriate for the fabulously wealthy.

However, a simple trust may only cost $2,000 to $4,000 in attorney's fees and can avoid both the expense and publicity of probate, provide a more immediate transfer of wealth, avoid some taxes, and provide you greater control over your legacy.

For instance, if you want to set aside some funds for a grandchild's college education, you can make it a requirement he or she enrolls in classes before your trust will dispense any funds. Like a will, beneficiary lines will override your trust conditions, so you must still keep insurance policies and other assets up to date.

Like any financial or legal consideration, there are many options these days beyond the "yes or no" of having a trust. For one thing, you will need to consider if you want your trust to be revocable (you can change the terms while you are alive) or irrevocable (can't be changed; you are no longer the "owner" of the contents). A brief note here about irrevocable trusts: Although they have significant and greater tax benefits, they are still subject to a Medicaid look-back period. This means, if you transfer your assets into an irrevocable trust in an attempt to shelter them from a Medicaid spend-down, you will be ineligible for Medicaid coverage of long-term care for five years. Yet, an irrevocable trust can avoid both probate and estate taxes, and it can even protect assets from legal judgments against you.

Another thing to remember when it comes to trusts, in general, is, even if you have set up a trust, you must remember to fund it. In our forty years' work, we've had numerous clients come to me, assuming they had protected their assets with a trust. When we talk about taxes and other pieces of their legacy, it turns out they never retitled any assets or changed any paperwork on the assets they wanted in the trust. So, please remember, a trust is just fancy legal papers if you haven't followed through on retitling your assets.

Taxes

Although charitable contributions, trusts, and other tax-efficient strategies can reduce your tax bill, it's unlikely your estate will be passed on entirely tax-free. Yet, when it comes to building a legacy that can last for generations, taxes can be one of the heaviest drains on the impact of your hard work.

For 2017, the federal estate exemption was $5.49 million per individual and $10.98 million for a married couple, with estates facing up to a 40 percent tax rate after that. In 2020, those limits have increased to $11.58 million for individuals and $23.16 million for married couples, with the 40 percent top level gift and estate tax remaining the same. Currently, the new estate limits are set to increase with inflation until January 1, 2026, when they will "sunset" back to the inflation-adjusted 2017 limits.[40, 41] And that's not taking into account the

---

[40] Ashlea Ebeling. Forbes. December 21, 2018. "Final Tax Bill Includes Huge Estate Tax Win for the Rich: The $22.4 Million Exemption." https://www.forbes.com/sites/ashleaebeling/2017/12/21/final-tax-bill-includes-huge-estate-tax-win-for-the-rich-the-22-4-million-exemption/
[41] Ashlea Ebeling. Forbes. November 6, 2019. "IRS Announces Higher Estate And Gift Tax Limits For 2020." https://www.forbes.com/sites/ashleaebeling/2019/11/06/irs-announces-higher-estate-and-gift-tax-limits-for-2020/#18b9e5652efb

various state regulations and taxes regarding estate and inheritance transfers.

Retirement accounts are also on the list of tax concerns.

Your IRA or 401(k) can be a source of tax issues when you pass away. For one thing, taking funds from a sizable account can trigger a large tax bill. However, if you leave the assets in the account, there are still required minimum distributions (RMDs), which will take effect even after you die. If you pass the account to your spouse, he or she can keep taking your RMDs as is, or your spouse can retitle the account in his or her name and receive RMDs based on his or her life expectancy. Remember, if you don't take your RMDs, the IRS will take up to 50 percent of whatever your required distribution was, plus you will still have to pay income taxes whenever you withdraw that money.

Thanks to rules enacted in 2020, anyone who inherits your IRA, with few exceptions (your spouse, a beneficiary less than ten years younger, or a disabled adult child, to name a few), will need to empty the account within ten years of your death.

Also—and this is a pretty big also—check with an attorney if you are considering putting your IRA or 401(k) in a trust. An improperly titled beneficiary form for the IRA could mean the difference of thousands of dollars in taxes. This is just one more reason to work with a financial professional, one who can strategically partner with an estate planning attorney to diligently check your decisions.

Two of our clients, a couple in their sixties we'll call Jan and Jeff, had come in to have Aaron do their estate planning work, complete with a Roapmap to Retirement financial plan—which was really convenient for them to be able to do all under one roof. A couple months after doing the work for them, we received a call that broke our heart . . . Jan called in and told us Jeff had cancer. We were all taken back, as Jan and Jeff had become like family to us. After hearing that news, it was clear to us just how important having an estate plan really is.

We are so happy to report that Jeff is now recovering, with the cancer in remission. This example just shows how having everything in order while times are good, while you have your health and wealth, is the best time to plan ahead for what could come.

CHAPTER 9
Finding a Financial Professional
by Bill Saoud

I got into the financial services industry right out of college after having seen my own family struggle with finances for so many years growing up. I often tell this story at my informational dinner seminars, describing how, after my mother passed away when I was six years old, our family dove into a tailspin. My father took charge of handling the family finances, and, frankly, he had a difficult time. So, as a young man, I wanted to help him in any way I could. I was fortunate to be able to provide him support in his later years once I opened my own business, now forty years ago.

I've now earned an insurance license, acquired a B.A. from Wayne State University, and have been working hard in the business for forty years. Aaron, my son, has earned his own B.A. from the University of Michigan; a JD from Stetson College of Law in St. Petersburg, Florida; he's licensed to offer investment advisory services; and insurance licensed in Michigan and Florida. He has also been admitted to practice law in Florida, Illinois, and Michigan.

We think people should not prepare their financial plans by themselves because it is imperative mistakes are not made and items are not overlooked when it comes to this most important part of planning for the rest of their lives. Nothing could be more important than making sure their families, children, and grandchildren are protected for the future.

We believe we are qualified to say this because we have been helping families for so many years, and there are so many things to consider when planning for retirement—taxes, insurance, investments, risk, and so much more. If you are planning your own retirement, it is likely you've never done anything quite like it before. And, if you make a mistake, there aren't any second-chances to retire. In unfortunate cases where mistakes are made, some people end up having to return to work if their retirement has not been planned for properly.

Retirement really does not look the same today as it did in years past. There are so many things to consider now: laws, rules governing your money, and, perhaps most importantly, the fact pensions and Social Security do not feel as much like certainties as they once did. There is an awful lot more planning that now has to be done at the individual level rather than at the government or employer level.

This increase in individual planning creates a larger need for the help of financial planners and professionals. We believe the three main things folks should look for in a financial professional are honesty, transparency, and experience. These three attributes are something that have been a top-down part of our company and mission concerning clients for decades, and we hold ourselves to the highest standards in these regards at Saoud Financial. We feel folks should demand the same of their advising office.

One of the easiest red flags to spot is a lack of integrity in the advisor and their staff when you meet them, whether at their office or out in the community. Do they look you in the eye and give you straight answers? Or do they appear to only have their interests in mind rather than always putting your best interests as their first priority?

We believe folks should come see us if they want help. At the end of the day, if a person or family acknowledges, "Hey, maybe

I shouldn't go this alone," then we know there is the possibility of our partnership being a good fit. I think of it much like my health care—when something is wrong, I can say to myself, "I am just going to ignore the pain in my chest, or take a few vitamins I read about online, and hope it goes away." Or, I can say more wisely, "My physical health is too important to leave to chance, so I am going to see a medical doctor or professional to make sure the pain in my chest is not something more serious." The same analogy can be applied to your financial health—I can read a few articles online, make a few stock guesses, and then hope my retirement works out okay. Or, I can seek out a professional to help me know for sure everything will work out well. And, maybe I might need to change my direction sooner rather than later, to avoid an undesirable outcome

The main thing we do at our office is give folks greater financial confidence. When families leave our office, they go home knowing what the future can look like, that they do not have to worry as much and that someone is watching out for them and their interests—with the assurance that they've prepared for a great future.

CHAPTER 10
Women-Specific Concerns

We help men, women, and families from all walks of life on their journey to and through retirement. Yet, we want to address the female demographic specifically. Why? To be perfectly blunt, women are more likely to deal with poverty than men when they reach retirement. One report notes nearly two-thirds of the 7.1 million older adults living in poverty in the United States are women.[42]

The topics, products, and strategies we cover elsewhere in this book are meant to help address retirement concerns for men *and* women, but those kinds of statistics are a reminder much of traditional planning is geared toward men. Male careers, male lifespans, male health care. The bottom line is women's career paths often look much different than men's, so why would their retirement planning look the same?

We think women's concerns should be addressed as their own chapter because we see, now, how much of a more significant role and impact women can and have been having on their family's finances. Whether taking control of the regular, day-to-day tracking of expenses or being the primary income-earner in the household, women have been taking on greater responsibilities than ever before. Unfortunately, during

---

[42] Liz Seggert. Association of Health Care Journalists. January 8, 2019. "New Report Paints a Grim Picture of Older Women in Poverty." https://healthjournalism.org/blog/2019/01/new-report-paints-a-grim-picture-of-older-women-in-poverty/

some women's lives, they were never given the tools or the attention to succeed in this area. For many years, this "wasn't a woman's place"—which we think is just downright ridiculous. But, even still, too many offices out there tend to treat the concerns of women as less important or less imperative than those of their husband's. So, we at Saoud Financial are really trying to change that trend to a place of better equality.

Be Informed

It's a familiar scene in many financial offices across the country: A woman comes into an appointment carrying a sack full of unopened envelopes. Often through tears, she sits across the desk from a financial professional and apologizes her way through a conversation about what financial products she owns and where her income is coming from. She is recently widowed and was sure her spouse was taking care of the finances, but now she doesn't know where all of their assets are kept, and her confidence in her financial outlook has wavered after walking through funeral expenses and realizing she's down to one income.

Often, she may be financially "okay." Yet, the uncertainty can be wearying, particularly when the family is already reeling from a loss. While this scenario sometimes plays out with men, in our experience, it's more likely to be a woman in that chair across the desk, probably, in part, because of Western traditions about money management being "a guy thing." But it doesn't have to be this way. This all-too-common scenario can be wiped away with just a little preparation.

Talk to Your Spouse/ Work with a Financial Professional

While there are many factors affecting women's financial preparation for and situation in retirement, we cannot emphasize enough that the decision to be informed, to be a part of the conversation, and to be aware of what is going on with your finances is absolutely paramount to a confident retirement. With all of the couples we've seen, there is almost always an "alpha" when it comes to finances. It isn't always men—for many of our coupled clients, the wife is the alpha who keeps the books, budgets, and knows, to the penny, where all of the family's assets are—yet, statistically, among baby boomers, it is usually a man who runs the books. But, as time goes on, it looks like the ratio of male to female financial alphas is evening out. According to a Gallup study, women are equally as likely to take the lead on finances as men, with 37 percent of U.S. households showing women primarily paying the bills. Half of households also say decisions about savings and investments are shared equally.[43] Whether that's the way your household works or not, there isn't anything wrong with who does what.

The breakdown happens when there is a lack of communication, when no one other than the financial alpha knows how much the family has, and where. In the end, it doesn't matter which person handles the money; it's about all parties being informed of what's going on financially.

There are a lot of ways to open up the conversation about money. One woman we heard of started a conversation with her husband, the financial alpha, by sitting down and saying, "Teach me how to be a widow." Perhaps that sounds grim, but it was to the point, and it opened up what she said was a very fruitful conversation. The conversation opener we often hear is when clients come to our office. Whether it's the financial alpha or the financial beta who set the first appointment, couples sometimes have their first real conversation about money, assets, and their retirement plans in our office. The important thing about having these conversations isn't where, it's when . . . and the best "when" is as soon as possible.

---

[43] Megan Brenan. Gallup. January 29, 2020. "Women Still Handle Main Household Tasks in U.S.." https://news.gallup.com/poll/283979/women-handle-main-household-tasks.aspx

Spouse-Specific Options

One area where it might be especially important to be on the same page between spouses is when it comes to financial products or services that have spousal options. A few that come to mind are pensions and Social Security, although life insurance and annuity policies also have the potential to affect both spouses.

With pensions, taking the worker's life-only option is somewhat attractive—after all, the monthly payment is higher. However, you and your spouse should discuss your options. When we're talking about both of you, as opposed to just one lifespan, there is an increased likelihood at least one of you will live a long, long time. This means the monthly payout will be less, but it also ensures that, no matter which spouse outlives the other, no one will have to suffer the loss of a needed pension paycheck in his or her later retirement years.

While we covered Social Security options in a different chapter, we think some of the spousal information bears repeating. Particularly, if you worked exclusively inside the home for a significant number of years, you may want to talk about taking your Social Security benefits based on your spouse's work history. After all, Social Security is based on your thirty-five highest-earning years.

Things to keep in mind about Social Security spousal benefits:[44]

- Your benefit will be calculated as a percentage (up to 50 percent) of your spouse's earned monthly benefit at his or her full retirement age, or FRA.
- For you to begin receiving a spousal benefit, your spouse must have already filed for his or her own benefits and you must be at least sixty-two.
- You can qualify for a full half of your spouse's benefits if you wait to file until you reach FRA.

---

[44] Social Security Administration. "Retirement Planner: Benefits For You As A Spouse." https://www.ssa.gov/planners/retire/applying6.html

- Beginning your benefits earlier than your FRA will reduce your monthly check, but waiting to file until after FRA will not increase your benefits.

For divorcees: [45]
- You may qualify to withdraw an ex-spousal benefit if . . .
    a. You were married for a decade or more
    b. **and** you are at least sixty-two
    c. **and** you have been divorced for at least two years
    d. **and** you are currently unmarried
    e. **and** your ex-spouse is sixty-two (qualifies to begin taking Social Security)
- Your ex-spouse does not need to have filed for you to file on his or her benefit.
- Similar to spousal benefits, you can qualify for up to half of your ex-spouse's benefits if you wait to file until your FRA.
- If your ex-spouse dies, you may file to receive a widow/widower benefit on his or her Social Security record as long as you are at least age sixty and fulfill all the other requirements on the preceding alphabetized list.
    a. This will not affect the benefits of your ex-spouse's current spouse

For widow's (or widower's, for that matter) benefits:[46]
- You may qualify to receive as much as your deceased spouse would have received if . . .
    a. You were married for at least nine months prior to his or her death

---

[45] Social Security Administration. "Retirement Planner: If You Are Divorced." https://www.ssa.gov/planners/retire/divspouse.html
[46] Social Security Administration. "Survivors Planner: If You Are The Worker's Widow Or Widower." https://www.ssa.gov/planners/survivors/ifyou2.html

    b. ***or*** you would qualify for a divorced spousal benefit
    c. ***and*** you are at least sixty
    d. ***and*** you did not/have not remarried before age sixty
- You may earn delayed credits *if* your spouse hadn't already filed for benefits when he or she died
- Other rules may apply to you if you are disabled or are caring for a deceased spouse's dependent or disabled child

Longevity

On average, women live longer than men. Most stats put average female longevity at about two years more than men's. But averages are tricky things. Perhaps a more telling statistic is the fact more than 80 percent of U.S. centenarians, those over 100, are women. That means the vast majority of the eldest elderly are women.[47]

On one hand, this is a Rosie the Riveter moment. How fabulous are ladies? On the other hand, this reveals longstanding financial ramifications.

We have a lot of female clients who are now widowed, and they understand, first-hand, the fact most women will outlive their spouses. Recognizing this also makes them more cautious with their money and, generally, a bit more conservative.

---

[47] U.S. Census Bureau. Dec. 10, 2012. "2010 Census Report Shows More Than 80 Percent of Centenarians are Women."
https://www.census.gov/newsroom/releases/archives/2010_census/cb12-239.html

Simply Needing More Money in Retirement

Living longer in retirement means needing more money, period. Barring a huge lottery win or some crazy stock market action, the date you retire is likely the point at which you have the most money you will ever have. Not to put too grim a spin on it, but the problem with longevity is, the further you get away from that date, the further your dollars have to stretch. If you planned to live to a nice eighty-something, but you live to a nice one-hundred-something, that is *two decades* you will need to account for, monetarily.

To put this in perspective, let's say you like to drink coffee as an everyday splurge. Not accounting for inflation or leap years, a $2.50 cup-a-day habit is $18,250 over a two-decade span. Now, think of all the things you like to do that cost money. Add those up for twenty years of unanticipated costs. We think you'll see what we mean.

More Health Care Needs

In addition to the cost of living for a longer lifespan is the fact aging, plain and simple, means more health care, and more health care means more money. Women are survivors.
They suffer from the morbidity-mortality paradox, which states women tend to suffer more non-fatal illnesses throughout their lifetime than men, who experience fewer illnesses but higher mortality. Men experience less sickness in general, but they are more susceptible to death when they do experience illness.[48] So survival is on the side of the woman. However, surviving things like cancer also means more checkups later in life.

---

[48] Melinda Martin-Khan. Medical Xpress. June 10, 2019. "Why Do Women Live Longer Than Men?" https://medicalxpress.com/news/2019-06-women-longer-men.html

Widowhood

Not only do women typically live longer than their same-age male counterparts, they also have the tendency to marry men older than themselves. The numbers bear this out: Women are four times more likely to outlive their spouses than men.[49] In addition, 50 percent of women will become widowed by age sixty-five—and many may live at least another fifteen years or more on their own.[50]

We don't say this to scare people; rather, we think it's fundamentally important to prepare our female clients for something that may be a startling, *but very likely,* scenario. At some point, most women will have to handle their financial situations on their own. A little preparation can go a long way, and having a basic understanding of your household finances and the "who, what, where, and how much" of your family's assets is incredibly useful—it can prevent a tragic situation from being more traumatic.[51]

As if to underscore the point the financial services industry as a whole often underserves women in these situations, the report points to this: 70 percent of widows fire their financial advisors after their spouses die. [52] In our opinion, this is because many financial professionals tend to alienate women even when their spouses are alive. We've heard several stories of women who sat through meeting after meeting without their

---

[49] Women's Institute For A Secure Retirement. 2019. "Widowhood: Why Women need to Talk About This Issue." https://www.wiserwomen.org/resources/widowhood-fact-sheets/widowhood-why-women-need-to-talk-about-this-issue/
[50] Ibid.
[51] Lifetime Financial Growth. June 01, 2019. "Why Are We Unprepared for Widowhood?" https://www.lifetimefinancialgrowth.com/blog/why-are-we-unprepared-for-widowhood
[52] Mercer Partners Wealth Management. September 30, 2019. "Transitions." https://www.mercerpartnerswealth.com/p/transitions

financial professional ever addressing a single question to them.

We have had multiple women, who felt alienated by their current advisor, come to see us after their husbands passed away—they felt their opinion hadn't been heard for the past twenty or thirty years. Then, when the woman assumes charge of her finances, she looks for an alternative approach from us, an office that will listen and understand her concerns.

In our firm, when we work with couples, we work hard to make sure our retirement income strategies work for both people. No matter who is the financial alpha, it's important for everyone who is affected by a retirement plan to understand it.

We have a specific approach for widows that always begins with this question: How much of an active role did you have in managing your family finances? Were you in charge of keeping track of expenses? Or, maybe, were you in charge of the investments, too? Going through several questions about a widow's experience and the approach their family took to financial plans helps us to know where to begin.

Taxes

One of the often-unexpected aspects of widowhood is the tax bill. Many women continue similar lifestyles to the ones they shared with their spouses. This, in turn, means continuing to have a similar need for income. However, after the death of a spouse, their taxes will be calculated based on a single filer's income table, which is much less forgiving than the couple's tax rates. With proper planning, your financial professional and tax advisor may be able to help you take the sting out of your new tax status.

Caregiving

While 66 percent of caregivers providing unpaid, informal care for the elderly are women, women also provide more than 50 percent more services than the men who provide care. The majority of women who provide caregiving services for the elderly are still in the workforce. Yet, on average, female caregivers lose close to $325,000 in wages and Social Security benefits, without even accounting for the losses of health care benefits and retirement savings.[53] This also doesn't account for maternity care, homeschooling mothers, or women who leave the workforce to care for their children in any way.

We don't repeat these statistics to scare you. Estimates typically place the monetary value of unofficial caregiving services across the United States at around $150 billion or more. Yet, we think the emotional value of care many women provide their elderly relatives or neighbors cannot be quantified with a number. So, to be clear, this shouldn't be taken as a "why not to provide caregiving" spiel. Instead, it should be seen as a call for "why to *prepare* for caregiving" or "how to lessen the financial and emotional burden of caregiving."

We have many clients now thinking about being the "sandwich generation"—meaning they may end up caring for their own children (coming back to live at home after college) *and* their aging parents. This type of financial responsibility can create additional household stress if not properly prepared for.

Funding Your Own Retirement

Specifically because of the aforementioned reasons, women need to be prepared to fund more of their own retirements. There are several savings options and products, including the spousal 401(k). Unlike a traditional 401(k), where you contribute money to a plan with your employer, a spousal 401(k) is something your spouse sets up on your behalf, so he can contribute a portion of his paycheck to your retirement funds. This is something to consider, particularly for families

---

[53] Where You Live Matters. November 5, 2019. "The High Costs of Caring for a Loved One." https://www.whereyoulivematters.org/the-high-costs-of-caring-for-a-loved-one/

where one spouse has dropped out of the workforce to care for a relative.

Also, if you find yourself in a caregiving role, talk to your employer's human resources professional. Some companies have paid leave, special circumstance or sick leave options you could qualify for, making it easier to cope and helping you stay in the workforce longer.

Saving Money

Women need more money to fund their retirements, period. But this doesn't have to be a significant burden—women are better at saving, investing, and paying down debt, on the whole.[54] This gives us reason to believe, as women get more involved in their finances, families will continue to be better-prepared for retirement, both *his* and *hers*.

---

[54] Dori Zinn. Debt.com. December 18, 2018. "Women are Better Than Men at Money Management." https://www.debt.com/news/budgeting-saving/handling-money-women-better-money-management/

Acknowledgments

First, to our amazing wives and children, we love you and thank you for being the backbone of our families and helping us make our lifelong dreams a reality.

To our clients, we thank you so very much—it is through your shared experiences, stories, trials, and tribulations that we have been privileged to work towards financial independence for all of our clients. You have made us a part of your lives and a part of your families, and you have turned to us in good times and bad, allowing our company to grow and become a great success in our community. Without your loyalty and faith in us, Saoud Financial would never have been around this long, and we would not be able to continue to help people like you every single day.

And last, but certainty not least, to our staff. We are so proud of your dedication, hard work, and persistence in allowing us the support to continue to share our gifts and our knowledge with the world. Every day, we continue to learn from all of you—just as much if not even more—than you learn for us. For that, we are deeply appreciative.

WILLIAM SAOUD & AARON W. SAOUD
About the Author

William Saoud, President and CEO

Bill has dedicated his life to serving others; as a veteran of the financial services industry, Bill pulls from more than three decades' worth of experience to help his clients create and protect retirement income.

Bill has been in the insurance business since 1982. Today, he is a registered member of the National Ethics Association and his company, Saoud Financial, operates offices in Shelby, Michigan, and in Tampa, Florida.

Raised in Detroit in the 1960s, Bill and his wife, Pat, together have four children—and are now happy to spend time with their three grandchildren, as well.

Aaron W. Saoud, Wealth Manager

Aaron's deep understanding of the financial services industry allows him to help his clients navigate their financial goals with confidence.

Aaron started out his career doing corporate litigation throughout Florida, mainly out of Miami and Tampa, on behalf of some of the most well-known and largest financial institutions in the world.

After leaving the world of "big law" in 2015, with a substantial knowledge on the inner workings of these companies, he transitioned to assisting families with estate planning, investing, and wealth management.

Aaron spends his time helping families with estate planning, financial planning, and investing for long-term dreams. He takes great pride in the work he does for his clients. He has a passion for helping others and discussing financial topics at speaking engagements throughout the area.

Aaron was born in Michigan, and earned his Bachelor of Arts from the University of Michigan, and then continued on to earn his law degree in St. Petersburg, Florida, at Stetson College of Law in 2011. He is a licensed attorney and financial advisor.

Aaron is a big fan of art and travel and can frequently be found looking for the next chance to explore somewhere new.

www.ingramcontent.com/pod-product-compliance
Lightning Source LLC
Chambersburg PA
CBHW071417210526
45465CB00001B/422